Jim,

I hope you enjoy
reading some of these
'off-beat' stories. Merry
Christmas 2011!

Earl

THE DAY I (ALMOST) KILLED TWO GRETZKYS

THE DAY I (ALMOST) KILLED TWO GRETZKYS

...AND OTHER OFF-THE-WALL STORIES ABOUT SPORTS...AND LIFE

JAMES DUTHIE

John Wiley & Sons Canada, Ltd.

Library and Archives Canada Cataloguing in Publication Data

Duthie, James (James F.)
    The day I (almost) killed two Gretzkys / James Duthie.

ISBN 978-0-470-67778-0

    1. Hockey—Anecdotes. 2. National Hockey League—Anecdotes. 3. Canadian wit and humor (English). I. Title.

GV847.D88 2010   796.96202'07   C2010-900211-3

Production Credits
Cover design: Soapbox Design
Interior text design and typesetter: Joanna Vieira
Printer: Solisco Tri-Graphic
Author photo on front jacket: Lorella Zanetti
Author photo on inside back flap: Courtesy of TSN

John Wiley & Sons Canada, Ltd.
6045 Freemont Blvd.
Mississauga, Ontario
L5R 4J3

Printed in Canada

1 2 3 4 5 STG 14 13 12 11 10

ENVIRONMENTAL BENEFITS STATEMENT

Using 3753.26 lbs. of Rolland Enviro100 Print instead of virgin fibres paper reduces John Wiley & Sons Canada, Ltd. ecological footprint by:

TREES	SOLID WASTE	WATER	AIR EMISSIONS
32	**920**	**86,986**	**2,019**
FULLY GROWN	KILOGRAMS	LITRES	KILOGRAMS

It's the equivalent of :
Tree(s) : 0.7 american football field(s)
Water : a shower of 4.0 day(s)
Air emissions : emissions of 0.4 car(s) per year

To Cheryl, Jared, Darian, and Gracie
For your love and inspiration

CONTENTS

FOREWORD

By ROBERTO LUONGO

The first time I met James Duthie, he had me run over by a Zamboni.

I was playing in Florida with the Panthers, and James and his TSN crew came down to do a story on the relationship between my back up goalie, Jamie McLennan, and me.

It sounded like your typical feel-good story. I figured he'd probably ask me the same kind of fluffy questions we always get with features like that. You know, "How do you and Jamie help each other improve? Do you hang out together off the ice? Is it like a brotherly relationship?" Everyone loves those warm-and-fuzzy hockey stories.

Now, I knew James from TV, but I didn't know him personally at all. So he strolls into our dressing room that day, and says, "Nice to meet you, Roberto. Here's my idea for this story. We'll shoot all these funny scenes of Jamie acting like he's your slave—tying your skates, buying your groceries, spoon-feeding you dinner—but secretly, he'll be fantasizing about murdering you so that he gets to play more. And at the end, we'll do a dream sequence where he runs over you with a Zamboni and crushes you."

O... Kay.

Actually, I kind of liked it. Sure beats the "How did you feel out there tonight?" interviews we have to do after every game. Plus, I can act. Luongo doesn't rhyme with De Niro by accident. So we shot all these scenes in and around the dressing room, and then at the end of practice, he pulls out this life-sized dummy they bought from some movie company. They had it dressed in full Panthers equipment. It did look kind of like me, though the hair wasn't nearly as good.

So Jamie was riding the Zamboni, wearing this mock-evil grin. I did all the close-up shots of my face, looking terrified as the Zamboni approached (I nailed it). And then Jamie rode the Zamboni down the ice, and ran over the dummy.

I think the story is still on YouTube somewhere. It was hilarious.

A couple of years later, after I had been traded to Vancouver, James and I did a sequel, where I was having flashbacks of the Zamboni-crushing. It was more brilliant acting and special effects. James kept squirting water on my face to make me look like I was sweating, and I would roll my eyes back in my head like I was having some sort of seizure. Once again, Oscar-worthy stuff. Or at least a Golden Globe.

The point of all this is that Duthie is demented. He is a sick, twisted individual. And I like that.

I have always gotten along well with the media, and I try to answer all the questions they ask. But sometimes you do get tired of the same old stories and columns every day. "Why are the Canucks winning?" "Why are the Canucks losing?"

The media needs originals. James is one of those. His columns are just like that story we did in Florida: unique, funny, often twisted and an absolute blast to read.

He really does have to get over the Kournikova obsession, though. It's not going to happen. Have you seen yourself in HD, dude?

The only thing that bothers me about the book is that there aren't any columns in here about me. You think if a guy agrees to write the foreword for your book, you might have found something half-decent to say about him. But I couldn't find a word. Sure, Tim Thomas gets a whole column. Luongo? Not even a paragraph.

And after all I've done for him. It hurts, frankly. Not as much as getting hit by the Zamboni, but it hurts.

PREFACE

"So what's your book about, Daddy?"

My six-year-old daughter Gracie asks me this as I'm slapping away at my keyboard, simultaneously editing two columns: one about coaches who ask players to refrain from sex before games, the other a fictional interview with a monkey who predicts the outcome of Stanley Cup playoff series.

I don't like my chances of nailing this answer.

"Well, it's about a lot of things, Sweetie. It's about hockey, it's about other sports, it's about being a fan, being a Dad and... lots of silly stuff."

"Is there a princess in it?"

"Uhh, no, Babe. No princess. Though I do mention Anna Kournikova a lot."

"What about a dragon, Daddy? Or zebras?" (She loves zebras.)

"No, no dragons. But there are some scary things in the book. Like those jellyfish that attacked us in PEI. And the howler monkeys that wanted to eat Daddy in Costa Rica. Oh, and I mention Sarah Palin, too. She's terrifying.

"As for zebras, Cupcake. Well, I do talk about referees. We sometimes call them zebras because of the stripes on their shirts." (Lame, I know. But she's six, okay? I thought it was a cute tie-in.) She looks at me, puzzled. "I don't get it, Daddy. If you're writing a book, what's the story about?"

I'm starting to sweat, now. She's relentless. Mike Wallace in pigtails.

"Well... this book has a lot of stories, Gracie. It's kind of like that fable book Nana gave you. Except most of these are actually true. (OK, some of them.) The stories are about all sorts of cool things! Things Daddy has seen during his career as a sportscaster, things about sports that make Daddy mad, things that make Daddy laugh, stories about famous athletes Daddy has met. And some weird stuff Daddy just dreams up in his head."

"Is that Ovechkin guy in the book?" (Alexander Ovechkin is the only hockey player she knows, because her brother once got to play a video game against him, and didn't stop talking about it for, oh, nine months.)

"Yup."

"Tiger Woods?"

"Definitely. There are all kinds of interesting characters in the book, Pumkinface! Sidney Crosby, Wayne Gretzky, Tom Brady, Tim Thomas, Derek Jeter, Sean Avery, Anna Kournikova (*that's two mentions already, the Vegas over-under for the entire book is 437), Ray Emery, Chris Chelios, Evgeni Malkin, Patrick Roy..."

"Miley Cyrus?"

"Uhh... no. Oh, but Hilary Duff is in there!"

"It would have been a better book if Miley Cyrus was in it."

And with that final editorial declaration, she bounces off to her room, likely to stage another apocalyptic war between her Playmobile people and her American Girl dolls. (I don't try to understand it.)

Oh well. Truth is, whether you are six or 66, I can't really explain what this book is about. It is a decade's worth of whatever-happened-to-seep-into-my-brain that particular week. Many of the columns appeared on tsn.ca, some in *The Ottawa Citizen* and a few other newspapers, but there is also a bunch that no one has seen before. I had stored them away in my hard drive, thinking I might do a book someday (but deep down, figuring I was too lazy to ever get around to it. All hail the power of Red Bull!).

Don't look for any meaning in the order of the columns. They are neither chronological, nor categorized. I always like books where the next page is nothing like the last.

If there are any mistakes of fact in here, blame my assistants. Oh crap, I didn't have any. Then blame Google, my fact-checker of record. OK, blame me.

I'd like to thank my bosses at TSN, and all the boys at tsn.ca, for always letting me write about whatever the heck I feel like writing about, even when it has little to do with sports.

Thanks to my high school English teacher, Mrs. Scott, who was the one who told me to forget all the rules of proper grammar, and journalism, and to just write, "anyway I wanted, about anything I wanted." And to tell anyone who told me otherwise to "Screw off!" Mrs. Scott ruled.

Thanks to my beautiful family, for putting up with me writing at the oddest of times, and in the oddest of places— hockey rinks, dance classes, water parks (don't ask). And for letting me use so much of our private life in my writings. You guys will always be my greatest inspiration.

Thanks to the athletes who, either by their amazing feats or their complete idiocy, provide endless fodder for a sports columnist.

Thanks, in advance, for the Nobel Prize of Literature, which will undoubtedly be bestowed upon this book.

And finally, thanks to Anna Kournikova*. Just because.

(*That's three, and the book hasn't even started yet. I smell a restraining order.)

IT'S ALL ABOUT THE SNACK, BABY!

December 2004

My son is facing the first heart-wrenching decision of his distinguished athletic career.

OK, so he's five. Just play along.

A scheduling conflict means he has hockey and soccer (indoor) at the same time Saturday morning. He must choose. Look, I know it ain't exactly Bo Jackson deciding between the Royals and the Raiders, but stay with me.

When I presented him with the problem, he paused pensively, clearly weighing his options. I could only imagine the conflict inside his soul:

"Do I don the armor of the rink warrior, feel the incredible surge of steel against ice and the pure primal joy of watching the black saucer come off my stick and press the mesh? Or do I choose the simple, beautiful game of foot on ball; the visceral thrill of bending one like Beckham past the helpless sprawling keeper?"

After a long silence, he responded:

"What are the snacks?"

"Ah...Wha...What do you mean?"

"Which one has the better snack?"

Oh.

Right. The Snack. The single greatest motivation of the child athlete. In the pros, it's all about The Ring. In tyke, it's all about The Snack.

My boy could score a natural hat trick in the final minute to win the league championship, but if there's no Kool-Aid Jammer waiting in the dressing room, he will curl up in the fetal position and weep.

I have seen kids play a full soccer game without getting past "fat-guy light-jogging" speed, then run a 4.2-forty across the field to snag a pack of Fuzzy Peach Maynards.

During one hockey game last month, our team's parents realized mid-game that due to some snack schedule snafu... the dreaded "Snackfu"... no one had brought The Snack. This caused sheer panic and fear in the stands. We all envisioned a team revolt, which would undoubtedly end in tears, tantrums, and in all likelihood, parental bloodshed.

Cameron (4): "Where's my f*&#!$'in Jooooooooce-boxxxxx!?!"

Dylan (5): "It was Jared's Daddy's turn! That b@$&* screwed me out of a Rice Krispy Square! Get him!"

Me (39): "Oh God! Please... No! Help Meeeeeeee!"

Lord of the Freakin' Flies. With skates.

A clearly terrified mother made a desperate run to Loblaws for those mini cheese and cracker thingys. She got back just in time. It was truly heroic.

We never had snacks when I played sports as a kid. Oranges, baby. It was all about the oranges.

I try to tell my kid that, and he looks at me like I'm a caveman.

"You ate oranges for The Snack? Was that before or after you discovered fire?"

My wife is a health nut. She wanted to do that Norma Rae thing, you know, make a snack stand. When it was our turn for The Snack at hockey, she wanted to bring bottled water, and apples or carrots or broccoli or... something sadistic like that.

My son was ready to walk right there. He was out of the family. He was prepared to put his face on the milk carton. Dude, your parents bring vegetables for The Snack? You are done. Your joyful boyhood is over. You won't see the puck/ball all season. It's a lifetime of atomic wedgies.

One Dad brought full-size ice-cream bars and Bibo Juice for The Snack (Bibo is very big. It's the Red Bull of the JK-SK crowd.). He was God. He had 11 kids ready to do anything he asked. This must be how cults get formed.

In the end, my kid chose soccer this weekend. Hockey is just a practice, and there is no guarantee of The Snack after practice (which he and a group of friends are actively lobbying to change). He figures soccer is a sure thing.

But just in case, he wants me to bring The Backup Snack. He developed the concept of The Backup Snack after that near miss at soccer last summer. It's a safety in case the designated snack parent fails to show.

The kid is good. It's only a matter of time before he has a Snack Agent.

"Look, he gets the chocolate-covered oatmeal bar or he doesn't dress, got it? He doesn't do plain or marshmallow!"

• • •

Postscript: He's 10 now. His hockey coach has banned the snack, but they still have it in soccer. We brought Freezies recently and I forgot to put ice in the cooler. They melted. He almost filed for emancipation on the spot.

10 THINGS YOU DIDN'T KNOW ABOUT SID THE KID

June 2008

Detroit is leading Pittsburgh 3-2 in the Stanley Cup Final.

• • •

Oh, no. Not another Sidney Crosby column. Enough already! Seriously, what is there left to say about the kid who has had more written about him than Obama and Brangelina combined? He is on the cover of *The Hockey News* every second week. They've written about him in *GQ, People, Men's Fitness* and every major sports magazine on the planet, outside of *Cricket Weekly*. A Google News search turned up 12,805 stories on Crosby in the past week.

But wait. How can you not write about the central figure in hockey's biggest event, right before a must-win game? So instead of repeating the ultra-obvious, the "He needs to have another great game tonight" stuff, I set out to discover 10 things you don't know about Sidney Crosby.

No. 1: One of his nicknames in the dressing room is "Creature," a nod to his freakish lower body. It is huge. Gigantic. Hugantic. His caboose would make J-Lo jealous. His thighs are bigger than my torso. All his pants have to be custom made. And the scary part is, his upper body is starting to catch up.

Sid's other nicknames in the room are now entirely related to his facial hair struggles. They include "Three-Beard," "Zorro" and "Greasy Mexican" (political correctness is not a forte of NHL dressing rooms).

No. 2: Sid can fight. We've seen him do it only once in his career (against Andrew Ference this year), but his self-appointed trainer, Georges Laraque, says any fool who decides to drop the mitts with Crosby better watch out.

"He came to me last year after I'd shown a couple of the other guys how to defend themselves properly in a fight. He wanted to learn. I was showing him some stuff and we were going at it, and I couldn't move him, he's so strong. He'd be really tough to fight."

So, did you pop him one, Georges? "Are you nuts? I value my career."

No. 3: Sid is superstitious. OK, this one you may have heard. But the extent of his superstition is as extreme as his skill. For instance, when he walks through the Mellon Arena, he has a specific route that defies logic.

"He will walk 20 yards out of the way to go around a certain pole or go through a specific door. And it never, ever varies," says one Penguins staffer, who showed me the route. It was baffling.

He also won't wear proper shoes in the dressing room. If he's showered and fully dressed, and has to go back into the room, he'll take his dress shoes off at the door, as if it were some traditional Japanese restaurant. When he eats, Maxime Talbot must sit on his left, Pascal Dupuis on his right. At a recent team breakfast in Detroit, a Penguins staffer sat down to eat, and was met with shocked stares from the players sitting around him.

"That's Sid's seat!" they said.

"He wouldn't have gotten mad or anything, he's too nice for that," says the seat-stealer. "But if I would have stayed there, he just would have hovered around quietly until I left."

Oh, and he raises his legs and touches the window when driving over railway crossings, but who doesn't do that?

No. 4: Sid might be moving. After three years living in Mario Lemieux's house, Crosby has started looking for his own place. Good thing, as I was about to give him another nickname: Kato Kaelin.

No. 5: Sid is not a health-food freak. The other day after practice, we chatted while he ate an ugly, white bread, mystery-meat, mayo-laden sandwich.

"You sure that's good for you?" I asked.

"You must have me mixed up with Robs (Gary Roberts)," he said, laughing. "I'm not picky. When I'm hungry, I eat."

"I'm working on him," says Roberts. "He came to my house last summer for a few days to train, and one night I made him this gra-nola, flax-oil, yogurt snack before bed. The next morning, he looked like hell. He'd been in the bathroom all night. Didn't go down so well."

No. 6: Sid understands the media better than Marshall McLuhan.

"It's crazy how smart and savvy he is," says Penguins defenseman Hal Gill. "Sometimes he'll say to us, 'The media is trying to write a certain story, so when they ask you this question, answer it this way.'"

Hey, wait a second! Maybe he's doing that to me right now. Evil genius, that Crosby.

No. 7: Sid is not always the "quiet" leader.

"When we lost that one game to the Rangers, he spoke to us about it," says another Penguins teammate. "He let us know we hadn't played our game. He did the same after Game 1 of the final. He just told us to relax. He doesn't do long speeches, but he knows when to speak up."

No. 8: Sid loves to kill bad guys. Sorry, I should clarify. I mean in video games. Last season, eight of the Penguins got PSPs so they could play a shoot-'em-up army game called SOCOM against each other. The guys were supposed to play only on planes, but it soon became clear that Sid was practising at home.

"Of course he had to beat all of us," says Laraque. "He's so competitive."

They've now moved on to "Call of Duty" on Xbox.

"He plays like a girl," says Talbot. "He's always hiding in the corner. Anything to win."

No. 9: Sid does anything to win because he hates losing. At Sunday dinner at a friend's house, he lost a game of Bingo to the friend's nine-year-old son. His instant reaction was to slam his first on the board, sending tiny bingo markers flying in all directions. He then blushed and laughed. But make no mistake, the reaction was genuine.

No. 10: This is the most important game of Sid's life.

Oh, wait, that part you knew.

• • •

Postscript: The morning the column was published (the day of Game 6 of the final), Sid spotted me in the hallway outside the Penguins dressing room and smiled. "You dug up some dirt on me, eh?" he said with a laugh. "Pretty accurate, I gotta admit."

His Penguins lost the game and the Stanley Cup that night. They would get their revenge one spring later, beating the Red Wings in seven games. Crosby hurt his knee in the second period of Game 7 and came back only for one shift. I interviewed him after the game and I have never seen a face so happy and eyes so glassy. The combination of joy, painkillers and champagne had turned Sid into one delirious mess.

THE FINAL TOLL

September 15, 2001 (four days after the terrorist attacks on New York City)

• • •

We, in sports, seem determined to attach a number to everything, and the nightmare of September 11 is no different. The "Sports World," this imaginary bubble we supposedly live in, lost LA Kings scouts Ace Bailey and Mark Bavis.

Two.

A neat, tidy death toll, perfect for the tickers at the bottom of the screen. But wrong.

We also lost:

Soccer moms, and Little League dads, and big sisters who became corporate bigwigs, but could still whip you at 21 when they came home for Thanksgiving.

We lost star shortstops from the corporate softball league, and secretaries who didn't play, but always brought the oranges, and cheered like you were Derek Jeter.

We lost 11-year-old boys who could have been the next Jordan or Gretzky, and four-year-old girls who could have been the next Mia Hamm or Serena Williams, not to mention whom they could have become in the *real* world.

We lost fans.

We lost Mets fans and Yankees fans, and fans who couldn't stand either, which was a damn brave stance in New York.

We lost Jets fans who'd always go to the game with the same three buddies, each shirtless with a big green painted letter stretching from navel to neck. And no matter how cold, they'd remain skin to the wind, screaming: "J-E-T-S, Jets!" Even when it was 21-3 Colts.

We lost bosses you couldn't stand, until they invited you to the box at the Rangers game and you both wore your Messier shirts, and forever bonded.

We lost girlfriends who left you alone on Sunday afternoons in the fall, or better yet, sat right next to you and cursed like a convict when Kerry Collins threw a pick.

We lost guys from the mailroom who'd spend a couple days' wages to sit in the nosebleeds with their girl at a Knicks game, and stockbrokers in Boss suits who'd spend a couple grand to impress a model with courtsides. But they'd cheer just as wildly. New York has great fans.

We also lost Red Sox fans, Bruins fans, Patriots fans, Capitals fans, Redskins fans, Wizards fans, and probably at least a fan or two for every team out there. Even the Bengals.

We lost fathers who'd take you to Mini-Putt and blow a six-inch gimme on 18 every time to lose by one, so he'd have to take you for ice cream yet again.

We lost mothers who somehow found time to run households with a bunch of kids, corporate divisions with hundreds of employees, and marathons in under four hours.

We lost Grampas who took you out for your first round on a real course, and pretended they didn't see when you teed it up on the fairway.

We lost coaches who'd work 60-hour weeks, and then spend their Saturdays trying to teach six-year-olds to stay in position, and not all chase the same ball.

We lost entire lines from the Firefighters Shinny League.

And you know what the saddest part of all is? Sport was just a tiny part of who these people were.

We lost *all* of them.

• • •

Postscript: I was hosting TSN SportsCenter *the day the planes hit the towers. We debated all day whether we should do a sports highlight show on a day when sports could not have mattered less in our world. We ended up doing a very sombre half-hour, mostly reaction to the tragedy from prominent athletes, and reports on how the various sports leagues would be cancelling games. I struggled for days to figure out how, and if, sports mattered in all this madness. Out of that, came this column.*

THE LONELIEST GUY IN THE RINK

October 2006

> *I looked up and you were there, just sitting there all alone*
> *At the lonely end of the rink, the lonely end of the rink.*
> —The Tragically Hip

Quick, kids. Name the most useless, irrelevant position in sports.

Point After Holder for the Buffalo Bills? Valid, but no. Post-Season Ticket Co-ordinator, Toronto Blue Jays? Close. Personal trainer John Daly? Sorry.

Try NHL Goal Judge.

Oh sure, once upon a time he was Da Man! Any goal the referee didn't see clearly, he would have the final say. His thumb, and that little red-light button, would decide the outcome of many a game.

Then along came two referees, overhead cameras, side-angle cameras, net cameras and video review judges. Suddenly, the guy behind the glass was forgotten. Yes, video killed the Radio Star. And the Goal Judge.

He is way-old technology. He's a Commodore 64. He's a Walk-man. He's VHS. No wait, worse! He's Beta.

"Oh yeah, we're obsolete. I mean they have 87 different angles on replay! They aren't going to ask us!"

His name is Bill. He has been an NHL Goal Judge for a dozen seasons. He didn't want his last name to be used. (OK, truth is he happily gave me his last name. It just sounds way more investigative when they don't let you use their last name.)

Bill Bedsworth takes his job as judge seriously. So seriously, in fact, that he actually *is* a judge. That's right, by day he's the Honorable Justice William W. Bedsworth, of the California Court of Appeal, one level below the Supreme Court. And by night, he's the Honorable Goal Judge William W. Bedsworth, of the Anaheim Ducks.

He prefers you just use his nickname: Beds. (You gotta love a high-level judge who wants to be called Beds. If I ever go to trial in California... like for... say... I dunno... stalking Scarlett Johansson... I want Beds as my judge.)

Beds is a lifelong hockey fan who has been a Ducks goal judge since the team's first game 14 seasons ago. Now he sits in the stands like some jilted lover, waiting, hopelessly, by the phone.

"They (the referees) used to call you back when they weren't sure if a puck went in. They never call anymore."

And this year, it will get even worse for goal judges. Most teams have moved them out of their little glass boxes behind the net, and banished them to Bob Uecker territory.

I was at a pre-season game in Vancouver last week, and the goal judge was higher than any human in the building, right under the catwalk. Binoculars will soon be mandatory equipment.

Beds has also been displaced. But he is hardly bitter. In fact, he's downright giddy he's gotten away with doing this dream gig this long.

"Even before, I was never in the right position to make a call! You should be positioned over the goal line. You know that. I know that. Tennis knows that, but hockey never did!"

Over the years, that bad angle caused him to light the lamp early a handful of times. Premature Illumination. Always embarrassing.

"Sometimes the puck would pop up, hit the side of the net, but you see puck hitting twine, you hit the light, and then it bounces off into the corner, and you go 'Oh God No!'

"But you try seeing past JS Giguere! I long for the days of goalies the size of Darren Pang."

Gretzky gave him nightmares. When The Great One was in his "office," the goal judge could see nothing from his. Grant Fuhr once chucked a water bottle at him when he disagreed with a decision. But nobody gets angry with the goal judge anymore. Heck, most have forgotten he even exists.

"I had a guy ask me if I was the security guard for the camera behind the net," Beds says with a chuckle.

He now sits in a regular seat, passing beers and popcorn down the row.

"Hey, dude with the phone, could you order me some nachos and two Bud!"

And yet Beds still feels he has a crucial role.

"I make the game more fun for the crowd," he pleads. "When a goal goes in, maybe 1,000 see it, and 16,000 don't." (Canadian fans may insert snicker here.) "Most fans have to wait to see that red light on before they can celebrate or want to commit suicide. They depend on us."

Amen, Beds. You're right. We still need you. That red light is a vital part of our hockey culture. (And in Dan Cloutier's case, a very regular part of it.)

So all rise for The Judge! Then sit back down. You're probably blocking his view.

• • •

Postscript: Beds has officially retired from goal judging, but still presides in his California courtroom. At the time of publishing, only three NHL teams still have goal judges behind both nets or in the Zamboni area (Boston,

Ottawa, Florida). Three have one judge still in the Zamboni area (Edmonton, Vancouver, Nashville). The other 24 teams have their goal judges spread all over their arenas. They are usually high in the nosebleeds, squinting to see if the puck crossed the line so they can hit their button and turn on the red light, knowing full well the Video God in the sky will have the last word anyway.

CANADA DAYS

March 2010

If you went to Vancouver for the Olympics, you probably get asked the same question I do, every single day. "What will you remember most?"

I know what they're expecting to hear.

Alexandre Bilodeau hugging his brother after winning Canada's first gold ever at home. Or Jon Montgomery strolling through Whistler after winning his gold, parting a sea of screaming fans like he was Moses (though I don't believe Moses wore a toque and swigged from a pitcher of beer). Or Joannie Rochette's courageous bronze, days after her mother's sudden death. Or wait, Sid! C'mon, surely he'll say Sid's goal!

All great answers. None right.

What I'll forever remember about Vancouver begins with a woman named Sylvie, who works behind the meat counter at a Robson street grocery store. She gave me the first clue this might be a very special time in this city. In this country.

The day I arrived, exactly a week before the Opening Ceremony, I went for a run in Stanley Park. This is my own Vancouver tradition—something I did every day when I lived there in the late 90's, and still do every time I come back. The Seawall in Stanley Park has to be in the top ten places to run on the planet.

So I get about 50 minutes in when I realize:

a.   I haven't run for 50 minutes in two years and am about to require paramedics.

b.   I haven't eaten since breakfast, and am prepared to bite the head off a chipmunk if one crosses my path.

So I limp back towards my hotel, stopping at a grocery store/deli called Caper's, which my wife and I used to frequent when we lived in Van.

Just to paint you a complete picture, I am wearing long black shorts (an early sign these would be very unusual "Winter" Olympics), a ripped long sleeve grey sweatshirt, and a ball cap on backwards. Put it this way, if any crimes had been committed in the area recently, I would likely be picked up for questioning.

I order a giant burrito, a smoothie, and a scone from their deli, and am well into all three by the time I get to the cash to pay. I had stuffed a 20 inside my sock before I left (I know—gross—hey, I'm a guy—what do you want?) But sure enough, I reach down, and it's gone.

So there I stand, sweaty and broke, with a half-eaten burrito in one hand, a half-empty smoothie in the other, and the scone and a couple of power bars sitting on the cash. Total: $18.70. Which is, according to my brilliant mathematical mind, $18.70 more than I have.

"Umm...Uhh...Geez...I have no money. And...no credit cards... and no ID to leave you...and I'm here for the Olympics...and wow... I'm really sorry," is about all I can offer the cashier.

An awkward 5 seconds or so passes until the woman behind me in line says, "I'll pay for him."

Hello, Saint Sylvie.

She works at the meat counter in the same store, and is buying a snack on her break. No, she doesn't recognize me from TV. I'm just a dude who looks like a really old skateboarder, with salsa dripping off his chin, in a bit of a pickle.

"You're here for the Olympics... we have to take care of our guests," she says, handing the cashier a twenty. "If you have time, come pay me back. If not, don't worry."

A Guardian Angel in a bloodstained apron. That small gesture began a month of pure wonder in Vancouver. I will never again in my lifetime see a city so darn... happy.

I grew up in Ottawa, where on Canada Day, the whole city comes downtown for a party. Well, the Vancouver Olympics was that same scene, with patriotism multiplied exponentially, 17 days in a row. Canada Days. Canada Daze.

Tens upon tens of thousands, filling the streets 18 hours a day. Every one, it seemed, in red and white, like they were on their way to form some giant human flag for a Coke commercial. (There was an occasional sprinkle of Dutch orange in the crowds. It didn't clash.)

As we strolled the jammed streets on the first Saturday night of the Games, one of my colleagues said, "This is going to get out of hand. People are going to get killed."

But somehow, it never got out of hand. These may have been the giddiest mobs in the history of mobbery (I don't care if it that's not a word).

We took the Skytrain to Alex Bilodeau's gold medal ceremony. On the 7-minute ride back, three separate renditions of "Oh Canada" broke out. For the entire Games, you couldn't walk three blocks without hearing it.

I had the night off when Rochette skated her long program, so we went to a bar to watch with a couple of friends. We were walking along Robson as the final flight of skaters started. About every fifth store or restaurant had a TV that was visible from the sidewalk. And in front of each of them, people stopped and watched, en masse.

It was a strange, wonderful scene. There were clusters of people, every hundred feet or so. It looked like a Busker Festival—*Must be a guy swallowing fire in the middle of that crowd! Is there a clown juggling chainsaws over there?* Nope. They were all watching the same thing. Thousands, all stopped dead in their tracks, as Kim Yu-Na nailed jump after jump.

Of course, this happened for every hockey game, too.

When Canada beat Russia in the quarters, playing the best single period we'll ever see any team play, I walked back from the rink, just to soak it all in (when you spent most of the Olympics in a TV studio, you get outside whenever you can).

I strolled past a guy wearing nothing above his waist except a large red "D" painted on his sizable belly (my best guess is that he'd been separated from his five friends wearing the C, A, N, A and A). He stopped, bear-hugged me, and said, teary-eyed, "This is the greatest night of my life!"

I was tempted to come back with, "I hope you don't have a wife and kids," but I didn't want to mess with his moment.

When Crosby scored to end the Olympics four days later, I instantly thought of my man D. He had a pretty good week.

Didn't we all.

Just before the overtime of that gold-medal game, a friend texted me from the Vancouver airport. He had just heard this announcement from a frustrated attendant: "This is once again the last call for flight 241. We are missing 49 passengers!"

Uhh, I don't think they're coming.

I'm in the hyperbole business. It's what we do in TV. We're always in a rush to proclaim something "The best game ever!" "The most dramatic ending of all time!" "A once-in-a-lifetime moment!"

But there is nothing I can say to oversell what happened on the streets of Vancouver for those two weeks. It was... magic.

I was aimlessly cruising YouTube the other day, and started watching videos of people celebrating Crosby's goal, and other Olympic moments, all across the country.

That was the first time it really kicked in: what we witnessed in Vancouver was also happening in Toronto, Tofino, and Truro.

I keep wanting to tell people: "Man, you should have been there. You should have felt it!"

Now I get it. You did.

• • •

Postscript: Sylvie wasn't working when I came back to see her two days after she'd bailed me out. I left a 20 and a CTV Olympic hat in a bag for her.

The people of Vancouver made these Games. Every volunteer, every police officer, every waiter and waitress... they could not have been better ambassadors.

I walked out of the International Broadcast Center with a German writer one day late in the Games. He was overwhelmed by how he'd been treated, "Do you Canadians ever have a bad day?" He asked.

Not many, especially in February, 2010.

PAULINA AND ME

February 2003

She was my first true love. Dad actually bought her for me when I was 16. *(Editor: What kind of sick freak of a father does this guy have?)*

She was older, sure, but we made it work. We'd spend countless hours together up in my room. *(Editor: What is this, American Pie 3? Hey, Stifler! Your Mom's at it again!)*

We'd just stare into each other's eyes. And then, after a few weeks, I'd put her down in the basement and wait until next year when we'd fall in love all over again. *(Editor: OK, wacko, who are you, Buffalo Bill? Call agent Starling!)*

Paulina Porizkova and I were destined to be together forever. *(Editor: Oh, I see. This is Fantasy Penthouse Forum.)*

She took me to beaches around the world, always wearing that seductive smile (and a lace-and-lycra bikini from Calvin Klein – $72).

But then I found the letters. It seems others were loving her, too. Gary in Milwaukee. Bob in Akron. Phil in Boulder. On and on it went. Each professing their undying love for my girl.

Bastards.

So it ended. She married that guy from The Cars (for all you kids, that was my generation's Kate Hudson and the guy from the Black Crows—it still makes no sense at all). And I moved on.

To Elle. And Kathy. And Heidi. And Elsa. And Yamila.

• • •

It's been 20 years since I got my first *Sports Illustrated* Swimsuit Issue in the mail. Still have it. Cheryl Tiegs is on the cover, white frilly suit drenched beneath a Jamaican waterfall. That day, as other teenage boys dreamt of becoming hockey and football players, I dreamt of becoming a Jamaican waterfall.

"Sizzling Cheryl Tiegs Beats the Heat," reads the caption. Not that anyone ever reads the caption.

Cheryl and I flirted, but I got serious only with Paulina. She graced the cover in 1984 ("Here Comes the Sun… Paulina Is in the Pink in Aruba"… a must-read) and 1985 ("Shaping Up Down Under… Paulina at Australia's Shark Bay"… a classic literary piece). I was smitten.

Forget December 25th; for a teenage boy, Christmas always came in late February.

An issue of *Playboy*, you had to sneak a peak at when the clerk at the Mac's Milk wasn't looking, but the *SI* Swimsuit Issue was acceptable reading material in our house. The only catch was getting to the mailbox before Dad. Or you might not get to read it until mid-April.

Sometimes you never got it. I would estimate that in the two decades I've subscribed to *SI*, I have not received the Swimsuit Issue roughly half the time. Since, to my best recollection, no other regular issue has ever been lost, I can only conclude that Posties dig Paulina, too. It's a wonder the *Victoria's Secret Catalogue* makes it through the system.

I dug through the dusty old boxes of *SIs* in my basement and found nine Swimsuit Issues, ranging from Waterfall Cheryl in '83 to "Yamila Sizzles in Mexico" in '02. Funny how they're in much worse condition than the regular issues, all torn and dog-eared.

Lately, every magazine seems to be on the swimsuit edition kick. *National Geographic* even has one. What's next? *TIME* – The Swimsuit Edition: The Women of Saddam?

I'll always be faithful to *SI*. Even if Paulina wasn't faithful to me. This year's issue is due to arrive any day. If it gets by the Posties.

• • •

Postscript: Last year, my Sports Illustrated *swimsuit issue went missing again. I was cursing the Posties, when my wife informed me that my son had picked up the mail a couple of days that week. I found it under his bed. I've never been more proud of him.*

THE DAY I (ALMOST) KILLED TWO GRETZKYS

June 2008

The first Gretzky I nearly killed was Wayne. Followed shortly thereafter by Walter.

That would have been some legacy: "Hey, it's the guy who took out Canada's greatest sports hero and its most beloved father in the same round of golf!"

I did it within two holes, too. I'm streaky that way.

The Great One was playing ahead of us in a practice round before his inaugural Wayne Gretzky Classic in Blue Mountain, north of Toronto. I figured it was safe to hit, with his group walking off the green on a par five, and me 230 yards back in the fairway. For I am to golf what Ray Emery is to punctuality. But just as a blind squirrel finds a nut once in a while, hackers occasionally connect, and suddenly my ball was flying right at 99 (in my panicked mind, it was specifically on a beeline for the left frontal lobe of his brain, likely meaning instant death). I'm not sure how long the ball was in the air, probably about five seconds (which is 4.9 seconds longer than the majority of my three-wood worm-burners), but it felt more like five months. I believe this was the precise order of my brain transmissions:

1. "Sweet... I crushed that!"

2. "Huh, that's sorta heading towards that guy in the red shirt."

3. "Wait, that guy in the red shirt is Gretz!"

4. "Oh crap, now it's going right at him."

5. "Well, I certainly enjoyed my career while it lasted."

6. "How fast can I get to Mexico?"

In what remains, without question, the greatest break of my life (and a predictable break in my golfing life), the ball hit just under the lip of the greenside bunker (and buried, of course), two feet short of The Great One. Since I didn't yell "fore," as fear had made me temporarily catatonic, Gretzky didn't see it coming. He must have heard the "Pfffff!" of ball meeting sand, as he stopped, and looked back briefly, likely screwing my next year's invitation.

For the record, I took two shots to get out of the sand, three-putted, and made seven. Happiest double ever. Sure beats prison, or being stoned to death by a nation of grieving hockey fans.

Walter's near-DBD (Death-by-Duthie) experience came one hole later. This particular manslaughter, I probably would have been acquitted of, because Walter almost gets killed on every hole.

You see, Walter wanders. He is the single nicest man on the planet, so he crosses tee-boxes and fairways constantly to talk to, sing to, dance with and sign autographs for, every single fan and volunteer on the course. He also likes looking for golf balls, which means if you are preparing to tee-off across a ravine, Walter is probably already in it, with a pocketful of Nikes and Titleists.

Canada's First Father was playing in our foursome, though it was sometimes hard to tell. The phrase "Where's Walter?" was uttered roughly 436 times in a five-hour round, roughly equalling the number of strokes taken by our group (my way of taking a shot at Gino Reda, without mentioning him. Oh wait. Oops.)

I was midway through a downswing when Walter's head popped above the tall grass about 20 yards in front of me, like a fox in a meadow. I made a Tiger-like mid-swing stop (the first and only time "Tiger-like" will ever be used as an adjective to describe my game, by the way), and Walter, thankfully, lived to sing and dance another day.

In reality, he would have been in much graver danger if he were in the woods 50 yards to the left of the fairway. Straight ahead is pretty safe territory when I'm swinging.

Just ask Fran Quinn or Brian Smock, the two amiable tour pros who were in my group (along with former NHLer Todd Harvey, one of the great characters in the game) for the first two rounds of the tournament. Quinn and Smock deserve PGA Tour Cards just for getting through 36 without breaking into giggles watching my bunker shots.

That's right, 36. This is no one-day corporate scramble, where you ride around on carts drinking Peach Schnapps. This is the real deal, a Nationwide (one step below the PGA) Tour Event. This is Canada's version of the Pebble Beach Pro-Am, except instead of Bill Murray and Ray Romano, you have Alan Thicke and the dude from Glass Tiger (God love our country!).

I really have no business being here. I'm guessing I was called only after Anne Murray, Ben Mulroney and the entire cast of Degrassi cancelled.

But it's some fun. There aren't many places you can have a beer with Brett Hull, Damon Allen and Charles Barkley (his presence guarantees you will never have the ugliest swing in the tournament).

It's like an episode of The Sports Surreal Life. Where else would you find your daughter playing tag with John Elway by the elevator? Or where your eight-year-old son can come running into your hotel room yelling: "Dad, today I saw Wayne Gretzky... and two frogs!"

I'm not sure which he thought was cooler. Give him a couple more years and he'll figure it out. For The Great One is amazing to watch at an event like this. He hosts the same way he played: brilliantly. He makes every sponsor, every golfer, every fan feel like he's having them over to his place for a barbecue. He must have signed

10,000 autographs here this week, including multiples for the professional "seekers" who stalk him everywhere he goes. They likely had their signed jerseys on eBay within an hour. But when Wayne's the host, he won't say no to anyone.

Good thing I didn't kill him. Or any other member of the gallery who put their life at risk by standing somewhere between me and the hole, no matter how obscure the angle. That was really my only goal for the tournament.

I missed the cut in the Pro-Am. Tough break for me. Good break for all members of the Gretzky family (Janet, Paulina and Ty were also playing) who may have gotten in my way.

• • •

Postscript: Somehow, Wayne did invite me back to his tournament the next year. It probably helped that when I saw him at the party the night after I almost murdered him, I said: "Sorry about Gino almost hitting you on that one hole. I told him not to hit yet... but that guy just doesn't listen."

HELL (GOALIE) WEEK

March 2005

There are a few things all hockey parents desire for their kids:

1. That they have fun.

2. That they learn about character and teamwork.

3. That they go in the first round, get max entry-level money and buy their folks a retirement cottage in Muskoka. (Relax, silly, you know I'm kidding. The Hamptons would be fine, too.)

And most important of all...

4. That they don't want to play goalie.

The most painful part of my brief two-season career as a hockey parent has been, without question, Goalie Week.

For the non-puckheads out there, house league teams in the younger age groups usually rotate the goalie each game, so every kid on the team gets a crack. I believe the LA Kings did the same thing this year.

Some kids love it and beg for the blocker and trapper for their birthday. Others will wish they had signed up for that crafts class at the library where you make caterpillars out of egg cartons.

Like my boy. This is his second year of hockey. He likes it, but still spends half his shifts trying to get the puck, and the other half counting the fluorescent lights on the ceiling. You know, kind of like Alexei Yashin.

But when I told him it was his Goalie Week, he looked like he'd just found out Scooby-Doo had been killed off in the season finale (probably got into Shaggy's stash and OD'd).

The kid was stressed. You see, his inaugural Goalie Week last year didn't go so well.

First, he could barely move in the equipment. Strapping pads to a 3-foot-7, 48-pound frame is like putting steel-toed boots on a pigeon. When he went down, there was no getting up. Some goalies play the butterfly. My boy played the possum. Plus, he didn't exactly have Pronger and Niedermayer in front of him. His team's Goals Against Average was 1.83. Oops, sorry, misplaced the decimal. I meant 18.3. They did lead the league in one category. Snow angels.

I think it ended 21–6 for the Red Team over our Blue Team (the Red team really loaded up at the trade deadline). My boy's save percentage was roughly .247, which I believe puts him just ahead of Jose Theodore.

There were a few moments of greatness. The possum technique can be effective on five-year-olds who can't raise the puck. And most Edmonton Oilers.

For months after that game, he had war-vet-type flashbacks, waking up in the night screaming: "Help!! Black rubber coming from all directions! Make it stop! Mommmmmyyyyy!!!!"

So when his number came up this year, he immediately started sobbing and shaking violently. OK, that was me. But he wasn't happy either.

Now, if this was one of those heartwarming ABC After School Specials, my boy would overcome his fears, make the game-saving stop in the final second, proudly declare that he now wants to be a goalie, and teach us all a valuable lesson about perseverance.

Ah... sorry. This time they lost 17-12, and as he walked past me coming off the ice, he made one of the most poignant, determined statements I'd ever heard him utter.

"Never again."

Is it wrong for me to say I hope he's right?

I now have the greatest admiration (or pity... it's a fine line) for parents of full-time goalies. And I thank the Lord (Stanley) above it will never be me. Goalies have the most pressure, and usually get the least exercise. And when they do succeed, they get jumped on by 15 other kids, and end up with a broken collarbone.

Plus, the equipment bag is roughly the size of the Grinch's sack after he cleans out Whoville. Seriously, this should be an event in the World's Strongest Man. Forget pulling the truck, boys, try getting from the parking lot to the dressing room with that sucker over your shoulder.

Goalie Week, I have concluded, is the hockey parent's equivalent of hazing. Trust me, when it's over, you feel like you've been shaved, tarred, feathered and taped to the net naked.

The other day, I bought him some hockey cards and he somehow got Brodeur and Luongo in the same pack with a bunch of no-name forwards. Pretty cool.

He kept the forwards. And gave the goalie cards to his little sister.

• • •

Postscript: My son is now 10, and a forward on his Atom rep team. He never played goalie again. Childhood scars are eternal. (And for that, I am truly grateful.)

YOU WANNA PIECE
OF ME!?!

April 2001

Time to indulge in a male fantasy. Sorry, this one does not involve
Jennifer Lopez and a jar of Skippy.

It's another kind. One of those inane, sophomoric trains of
thought that makes us proud to be male.

Warning: this is strictly for the high-testosterone crowd. That,
of course, includes most men and the Chinese women's swim team.

From the gender that brought you "So, How Much Ya Bench?"
we proudly present "So, Who Could Ya Take?"

It's simple really. Just like us. Name an athlete you think you
could pummel. Our inspiration is Philadelphia's new hero Chris
Falcone, the Cheesesteak who tried to go at it with Tie Domi in the
penalty box. In Philly, that's Purple Heart material. He'll likely get a
statue right next to Rocky's.

Sure he's a cement-head (he actually is a concrete worker, and
I've heard it does tend to get in your ear), but he does have guts (even
though on that night I suspect they were heavily coated with Bud).
And maybe in this age when the relationship between Pro Jock and

Joe Fan is more bitter than sweet, that Philly Fanatic was just acting out a new kind of fantasy. We used to dream about going one on one with Curtis Joseph. The WWF Generation dreams about going one on one with Matthew Barnaby. In a cage match.

So join me. Abandon your good sense and high moral ground for a few minutes. Find your inner–Edward Norton, and join this little fantasy Fight Club. Since there's no one else around, I'll go first. Feel free to play along at home.

Tale Of The Tape: I'm 5-foot-10, 170. In a soaked parka.

I've been in three full-fledged fights in my life. Two before Grade 5 and the other against a cat. I don't plan on anymore until I'm at least 80, grumpy and in a nursing home. At that point, if you steal my remote, or my one daily-allotted cookie, I will whale on you.

So, Who Could Ya Take? Frankly, hardly anyone. I'm a realist. And perhaps of more relevance, I'm sober. Put a six-pack in most males, and they will inevitably try to convince you they could go the distance with Roy Jones Jr.

"Seriously, man! I'd just juke and jive him. Juuuke... And Jiiiiive. He couldn't touch me!"

Still, there are a few guys I figure I could handle. Like goalies. Maybe not all goalies, but some. I've seen Ron Tugnutt shirtless in the dressing room. He looks like Ghandi. I might be able to take Tugger. (Of course, because he's about the nicest guy in the NHL, he'd probably let me. I could live with that.)

As far as position players, it's grim, though I do like my chances against either of the Bure brothers. I'd play headgames with them. Make 'em cry.

"Hey, Pav... wonder what Sergei's doing right now? Could have been you, Pav, could have been you."

"Hey Val, Full House sucked."

Football? Again, position players are essentially a write-off.

Flutie's smaller than me, but I couldn't catch him. I could probably hurt Rob Johnson. Apparently, anyone can do that.

Besides that, it's tough. Even the kickers are into the creatine these days. But unless he booted me in the shin, I know I could take the Bucs' Martin Gramatica. He looks like Gazoo.

I figure I could probably take a few of those portly baseball pitchers, too, though they are crafty. I hear Tim Wakefield punches really slow... it looks like its coming at your head then drops to your gut at the last minute.

The arms are just too long in the NBA. I'd have a shot against that human twig Shawn Bradley. But I'd have to use the Van Gundy technique, and bite his ankles.

That's about it for the big He-Man sports, unless you count golf. All these guys wearing slacks, whose names end with "III." Them, I could take.

And jockeys. I believe if they put the whips down, I could take every living jockey.

So Ron Tugnutt, the Bures, Martin Gramatica, Davis Love and friends and jockeys. Against anybody else, I'm turtling.

You do any better, tough guy?

By the way, you can also play Celebrity "So, Who Can Ya Take?" Example: Russell Crowe. No. Sheryl Crow. Maybe.

Now kids, we're not advocating more Falconian acts here, so please remain in your seats. This is pure Tuesday night beer and wings conversational machismo.

Though I must admit, there have been times, when interviewing some monster-ego superstar, that I wished I'd responded to one of his snippy comments with a more suitable follow-up question:

"You wanna go?"

• • •

Postscript: There are dated sports and pop-culture references throughout this book, but I'm not going to bother explaining them all. I want the columns to be snapshots of the times they were written. Besides, my buddy Scooter always said, "If you need to explain your jokes, they aren't funny enough." But I'll make an exception here. Anna Kournikova had broken up with Pavel Bure and was dating Sergei Fedorov. Val Bure is married to Candace Cameron, from Full House. *And Bills' quarterback Rob Johnson was getting hurt every second game. That's all I got. You're on your own the rest of the book.*

GROWING UP IN SECTION G

June 2002

It is Father's Day this week, and as usual, I have no idea what to get Dad (do they serve brunch at Hooters?). But I do know what he wants. Sometime in late June, the CFL will announce whether football is coming back to Ottawa next season. Next to Mom and us, the Riders were Dad's life's passion. Getting them back... Now that would make his day. And it would sure beat the bottle of Lectric Shave I get him every year. As for a card, well, I'm not much of a Hallmark guy, so this will have to do:

Everything I know about life, I learned in Section G, Row 22, Seat 30 of Frank Clair Stadium. Most of it from the guy in Seat 29.

PASSION

I spent almost 20 years on that piece of plywood, right next to my Dad, shouting our lungs out for the Ottawa Rough Riders. They were, arguably, the 20 most miserable years any franchise in any sport has ever had. And they were the best times of my life.

Football was the first thing I ever really loved, with the exception of maybe Karen Andrews in Grade 3. She rocked my world. Well, as much as an eight-year-old's world can be rocked. That was puppy love. The Riders were the real thing.

PRIDE

My entire grade-school wardrobe consisted of two black mesh Rider jerseys: Number 7 for Conredge Holloway, Number 2 for Tommy Clements.

In the winter, I added a turtleneck underneath (don't say I can't accessorize, ladies).

Dad was worse. Shirts, sweaters, jackets, socks, gonch—if it had a big R on it, he wore it.

At some point, I got too cool and stopped wearing anything Rider. Dad never got too cool. Dad couldn't care less about cool. Dad was the true definition of fan.

FAITH

The Riders sucked. Boy, did they suck. They had bad players, bad coaches, bad owners, bad karma. Just to recap, they:

- once drafted a dead guy.

- once traded their first round draft pick... to two different teams.

- once sent a player to the locker room to get his injured knee shot up, and the team doctor shot up the wrong knee.

- once decided to move a practice across town, couldn't fit all the guys on the bus, left a few behind, and then forgot about them. I know this because I came across them, in full uniform, sitting on their helmets in the Carleton University parking lot, and had to give them a ride (there's frosh-week fun: how many football players can you fit in a Dodge Colt? Answer: five, with a DB in the hatch).

From 1980 to their demise in 1996, the Riders had a grand total of ZERO winning seasons (though we did get to .500 twice in a row from '91–'92, a period we simply call "The Dynasty"). And through it all, Dad still believed.

"This is going to be the year." (1-15)

"I really think they got a shot this week." (62-3 loss)

"This new kid could be the next Russ Jackson." (Charlie Weatherbie—he lasted seven games.)

His faith was seldom rewarded. Doesn't that make it even more admirable?

GIRLS

I don't remember when the cheerleaders became as important as the game, but I'm guessing it was when I was about 13. Dad brought binoculars every week, and I'd spend every TV timeout going up and down the dance line. Once I'd picked out my favourite, Dad would do the same, and then give me a "Don't Tell Mom" wink.

When I was 20, I dated a Rider cheerleader (her eyesight was bad) for, oh, about a halftime. Dad never said anything, but I think he thought that was pretty cool.

GENEROSITY

I loved baseball, too, so when I was 14, Dad bought me a Sony Walkman, so I could go to the Rider games and listen to the Montreal Expos. On the last Saturday of the 1981 baseball season, the Expos had a chance to clinch their first-ever pennant against the Mets. I seemed to be the only one in Section G with a Walkman (they were pretty new back then, a fact that officially qualifies me as an old fart). Before long, I was doing play-by-play for all the folks around me. When I described Wallace Johnson tripling home the winning run, Section G went nuts. I decided then and there I wanted to be a broadcaster.

Thanks for the Walkman, Pops.

LOVE

In all those years, we never once left a game early. The place would be empty as the clock wound down on another 55-7 massacre, and Dad wouldn't budge until :00. For years, I couldn't figure out why. I'm sure part of it was simply his unwavering belief that something good might actually happen, but there had to be more.

Then one day, not long ago, it hit me.

It was one of those perfect Sunday evenings, and I was playing with my 18-month-old in the park. He'd throw (some semblance of a throw anyway) his mini-football at me, I'd do the full Cuba Gooding Jr. touchdown dance, and he'd laugh like I was Richard freakin' Pryor. In those Kodak moments, just hanging out with your son watching him grow up, a father wishes he could call timeout and stop the clock permanently, so the game would never end.

My guess is, all those wonderful nights in Section G, Dad felt the same way.

• • •

But the clock did hit :00. In the last few years before the Riders died, I moved down to the sidelines to cover the team for a local TV station, and Dad moved to the swanky midfield section (I think he figured buying more expensive tickets would somehow help the team survive). He'd bring Mom or one of his friends, and sometimes I'd look up during a timeout and find him working the binoculars.

"The blonde, third from the end, is cute."

He couldn't see me, but I'd wink anyway.

HOPE

Dad's been retired for a while now, and spends most of the year at a cottage a couple of hours outside Ottawa. I asked him the other day if he'd still buy season tickets if the Riders were re-born.

"First in line," he replied.

He would be, too. Oh, and Dad, if it does happen...

Save me a seat.

• • •

Postscript: CFL Football did come back to Ottawa the next year in the form of the Renegades, a franchise that somehow managed to be even worse than the Rough Riders. They lasted four seasons before folding again. But Dad was first in line, and didn't miss a game. He now patiently awaits another CFL revival in Ottawa, which, at the time of writing, was still up in the air.

TAKING OUT THE TRASH

November 2007

In the wake of the nasty trash-talking incident between Sean Avery and Darcy Tucker last weekend, the National Hockey League knew it had to act.

After all, what kind of example does this set for our children? My six-year-old daughter saw Avery's antics on *SportsCenter.* The next day, she got in her best friend's face about how she dressed her Polly Pocket.

"You put the pink dress on her?!? Don't bring that weaka** fashion into my dollhouse! Go back to Barney until you're ready to play with the big girls, you JK bee-otch!"

Deeply troubling. (Though it did work. She got the girl totally off her game.)

The NHL wants its players to be role models. It has levied fines to discourage trash talking, but knows it needs to do more in the area of prevention.

Since totally eliminating verbal jousting in hockey is impossible, the league has instead produced a manual to instruct players what language and phrasing are acceptable during on-ice confrontations. The book, called *Let's All Be Friends! An Educational Guide to Proper On-Ice Etiquette in the National Hockey League,* will be distributed to every player in the league (*who can read) next week.

We have obtained an advance copy. Here are some excerpts:

SECTION 1.1 References to opponent's mothers:

Unacceptable: "You M!#*!*?#!**r."

Acceptable: "I understand you have a very close relationship with your mother. I must tell you this is a quality that I greatly admire."

SECTION 1.2 References to opponent's spouses/girlfriends:

Unacceptable: "Hey D*%*!#**e! Is that your woman? When did she break up the Rangers?"

Acceptable: "I must say, your life partner seems like a wonderful person with a good heart. And her posture is excellent."

SECTION 2.4 Pre-game banter:

Unacceptable: "You cross that centre line, I will rip your f#*%*#*%! eyes out. And even if you don't, I'm doing it on the first shift."

Acceptable: "Did you see *The Bachelor* last night? I can't believe he sent home Tina from Milwaukee! She was sooo sweet! Any who, good luck tonight!"

SECTION 3.5 Comments on opponent's hockey skills:

Unacceptable: "Hey jerkface! You're horrible! You skate like Snuffleupagus on Sesame Street on Ice! What is this, bring your minor-leaguer to work day?"

Acceptable: "Wow, your skating has really improved. And I must say that slap shot has impressive velocity. Do you do Pilates?"

SECTION 4.1 Comments on opponent's physical appearance:

Unacceptable: "Nice face, freak! You were great in *28 Weeks Later*! You make Ricci look like Clooney, you d%*#$!"

Acceptable: "Your face has a lot of character. And your skin is radiant. What moisturizer do you use? Oh, and when you get your teeth done, I know a great cosmetic dentist in Dallas. He did my veneers! Text me!"

SECTION 7.9 References to embarrassing off-ice incidents:

Unacceptable: "Hey Dirk Diggler, saw that photo of you on the Internet! Were you swimming before that was taken?"

Acceptable: "I really admire how you go to such lengths to connect with your fans."

• • •

Postscript: That last one, in case it slid past you, was in reference to former Toronto Maple Leaf Jiri Tlusty, who took some... uh... revealing photos of himself, which ended up being posted by the girl he sent them to. In retrospect, it was the most impressive thing we saw from the Leafs that season.

THE TERROR BENEATH

September 2006

OK, so the title is a stretch, but over-dramatizing is just what I do. And for the record, this column has nothing to do with sports. Except for one Brad Richards quote. Which is good enough for me. Look, I've been on holidays all summer. It's all I got.

So we're planning our Griswald summer vacation back in May and everyone we know chirps: "Go to PEI! You've got to go to PEI! It's Canada's Hamptons! Our secret paradise!"

Now, they were right, mostly. Gorgeous island. Wonderful people. Great beaches. But there was one teeny-weeny detail they left out. No biggie really. Just the BILLION BLEEPIN' JELLYFISH ATTACKING MY FAMILY!

You don't understand. This was biblical. Apocalyptic. It was like War of the Worlds. I half expected Dakota Fanning to come running past me screaming some cheesy line like "My puppy... They took my puppy!"

The first signs of impending terror came on the ferry over from Nova Scotia. As we were approaching shore, we started to notice all these hugantic red dots floating near the surface.

"What are those, Daddy?" asks my inquisitive five-year-old daughter.

Being the astute marine biologist I am, I answer: "Umm... those are... uh.... plankton mussels... or something... oceany like that, honey."

I really have to start reading more. Ah, who's kidding who. I really have to start watching Discovery more. Fortunately, there was this Captain Highliner–type character standing right next to us.

"Aye matey! Them's Giant Jellyfish!"

OK, he may not have really said "Aye matey," but he did have the white beard, and I believe he was concealing a pipe.

Big deal. Jellyfish. All part of the adventure, right? And besides, suckers that big can't possibly come close to shore.

Flash forward. Next day. North Cavendish Beach. Large hairy American man next to me in the water.

"Hey, neat! Look at that cool thing near my leg... OWWW!!#$% MOTHER OF @*$!*#! Mommy! I need my mommy!"

This scene would be repeated over and over. From the few words I could decipher between the curses and primal screams of victims, being stung by a jellyfish is roughly akin to having a wasp's nest shoved up your... ah... bellybutton.

The lifeguard at Cavendish tells us this is the largest jellyfish invasion anyone on the island has ever seen. He claims they usually show up only for a couple of weeks later in the summer, and even then, there is only a handful.

Thanks, Hasselhoff. So you're telling us we picked the single worst swimming week in the history of Prince Edward Island. Thirty freakin' degrees and sunny every day. Clear, crystal water, bathtub warm. And these gargantuan Jell-O Pudding Pops with four-foot-long stingers every second step.

Seriously, this could have been a Peter Benchley novel.

Granted, jellyfish are not the most cunning and elusive of sea predators. In fact, they move like Bengie Molina. From what I can tell, the travels of a jellyfish are dictated entirely by the current. They will bring you down only if you bump into them. Much like the Raiders defence.

I call NHL star Brad Richards, who still spends his summers in PEI, for emergency advice.

"Just grab them by the tops, and they can't sting you. You can pick them up and chuck them as long as you don't touch the tentacles."

Sure, Mr. Conn Smythe. Easy for you to say. I'd probably toss the queen jellyfish, causing the rest to hunt me down and latch on to my face, like the guy who orders the Nagafuki Surprise in that classic Bud Light commercial.

You know what they say. Hell hath no fury like a jellyfish tossed.

So I spend most of the week playing Chief Brody, scouring the shoreline with my binoculars, then screaming at my children to get out of the water if they are more than ankle-deep. Of course, you can't keep kids from anything that looks remotely like Jell-O. By week's end, my boy was bopping them on the heads with his plastic shovel, and my two-year-old daughter had taken to scooping up the dead jellyfish washed up on shore with a stick and dissecting them. I know. There may be issues there.

Anyway, we miraculously got through The Great PEI Jellyfish Invasion of '06 sting-free. And oh, the tales we'll tell future Duthie generations.

I believe this is where the Morgan Freeman closing voice-over begins.

"Eventually the jellyfish terror subsided. The carnage left behind, a reminder of mankind's fragility... (poignant pause)... but also... his perseverance. For humanity, as it has done through the ages, finds a way to overcome. To fight back. And ultimately... (longer poignant pause)... to survive."

Amen, Morgan Freeman. Amen.

• • •

Postscript: *I got a lot of e-mails from angry Prince Edward Islanders after that column, claiming I was going to ruin their tourism industry. So I should clarify that I now go back to the beautiful island every summer for Brad Richards' golf tournament, and the jellies aren't nearly as bad as they were that one terrifying summer. But I still won't go in the water. And I avoid the Jell-O at the Mandarin buffet. The psychological scars run deep.*

MIDDLE STANDINGS
SYNDROME

March 2008

When we were growing up, my sister, the second of three kids in the clan, used to chirp constantly about "Middle Child Syndrome." It was a long-running gag. She would accuse our parents of ignoring her while spoiling our oldest sister, the first born, and me, the baby.

I would respond by saying she was delusional as there were clearly no favouritess in our family. I'd do this while being cuddled in my Mommy's arms, being spoon-fed ice cream. I was 17.

The shrinks will tell you there is something to Middle Child Syndrome, and I do my utmost daily to make sure it doesn't affect my own middle child, little what's-her-name.

The NHL has its own version of MCS. Call it MSS: Middle Standings Syndrome.

Having your team in a playoff race is intoxicating, but losing out at the end has never been more devastating. Narrowly missing the Stanley Cup Playoffs has become the worst thing that can happen to a franchise. (Next to being owned by a pension fund.)

"It is (expletive) deadly," says one NHL general manager. "Mediocrity is a terrible fate in this league now."

Playoff teams get extra cash (the NHL range is roughly $700,000 to $1.3 million per home playoff game), tons of fan-buzz, more season-ticket renewals and a 1 in 16 shot at Stanley. And this year, 1 in 16 isn't far off the actual odds. In the parity era: you get in, you can win.

At the other end, NHL bottom-feeders get a lottery pick in the draft, which can turn a franchise around in one single selection. Be lousy for multiple years and you can set yourself up for the next decade. See: Washington (Ovechkin, Backstrom), Chicago (Toews, Kane), Pittsburgh (Fleury, Crosby, Malkin, Staal), and the former Sultans of Suck—Ottawa (Redden—via Berard, Phillips, Spezza—via Yashin, Daig... oops, sorry typo).

So being good is good, and being bad can be good, but being anything between good and bad... is bad. (Apologies if reading the preceding sentence gave you a nosebleed.)

"One year of just missing the playoffs, you can probably handle, but two or three years in a row can really cripple you," says another GM. "In our league now, you have to either capitalize on your talent, or capitalize on your lack of talent."

The Toronto Maple Leafs have become the poster boys for Middle Standings Syndrome. They finished 9th in the east the last two seasons, and are likely headed for something in the 10th to 12th range this year. Their perennial late-season charges are admirable from a hockey standpoint, but disastrous for the future of the franchise. The potential destiny-changing players they've missed out on the last two seasons include Kane, Toews, Backstrom, Staal, Sam Gagner.

We now pause briefly to let Toronto fans throw up.

OK, resume.

Erik Johnson (who looks like he will win a Norris or three someday), Peter Mueller, Nicklas Backstrom and soon to be added: Steven Stamkos, Drew Doughty and more.

The Leafs are not alone. The Florida Panthers also suffer from MSS. They are on the verge of their fourth straight non-playoff/non-lottery season, making a certain former Senators coach the star of his own sitcom: Martin in the Middle.

MSS doesn't have to be fatal. Teams such as Detroit, Buffalo and Ottawa seem to find impact players no matter where they draft. But it makes life much more difficult.

And draft position isn't the only issue for MSS teams. They may have trouble attracting big-name free agents, who usually prefer teams with either playoff pedigree or future potential. Places like Chicago and Washington, with their stock of young talent, will be just as attractive as Anaheim and Detroit this off-season.

It's hard not to feel a little sorry for Paul Maurice and his Leafs. They did exactly what they've been programmed to do their entire lives: play hard, and try to win as many games as they could. But as Morgan Freeman told Brad Pitt in *Se7en*, long before he found poor Gwyneth's head in a box, "This isn't going to have a happy ending."

As for you Leaf-haters, the joke has changed. You can no longer make fun of Toronto for being awful, like you did all those decades when they were. They're not awful. They are middling. Which, sadly for them, hilarious to you, is now worse than being awful.

• • •

Postscript: *Both Florida and Toronto did miss the playoffs that season, and Jacques Martin and Paul Maurice were soon fired. Toronto and Florida finally escaped MSS in 2009, when they finished 2nd and 3rd last overall, respectively. Alas, Toronto traded away its draft pick (as well its first-rounder in 2011) to Boston, for Phil Kessel.*

CONTROL FREAK

December 2001

I shut off the TV and, all stuffed full of myself, immediately think of Alec Baldwin in *Malice*.

"You're asking me if I have a God Complex? Let me tell you something... I am God."

Yeah! What he said!

So cocky, but oh soooo true. How can I not talk smack? What I've done over the past four hours or so is the stuff of legends. This was perhaps the most dominant performance of my career. Left! Right! Jump! Jump back! Up, up, up, up, up, up, right there! Crossover, jump back, down, down, down... Yes!!!

Unstoppable.

It's 11:38 p.m. on a Sunday, and I am Tiger. I am Gretz. I am Jordan (and I mean flying/tongue-wagging/in-his-prime/Chicago Jordan as opposed to bad knee/settle for jump shot/end-of-career Washington Jordan). I am all of them, except I'm in sweats and a six-year-old Gap T-shirt with a large mustard stain near the navel, lying horizontal on my couch.

I stand up, and coolly toss the TV remote down as I strut away to bed.

• • •

There are few things a man will truly master in his life. The remote, I have.

It has become an extension of my right-hand (I'm actually left-handed, but flick righty, a freakish abnormality). I know, you probably think you're Da Man, too. Most in our species are good at it. It's just who we are. It's what we do. But I'm a full-fledged phenom.

You wanna go? Stick that new plasma in the back of your SUV and come on over. Oh, we'll go all right. You got no shot.

I'm Monet with that thing. I've done four football games simultaneously without missing a play. I can do Letterman, Leno, Koppel and two west-coast hockey games without breaking a sweat. I can flick when one show goes to commercial, subconsciously time the break, and flick back within two seconds either way of show resumption. Often, I'll return right in those few frames of black between the last commercial and the first scene. That's called the Seamless Flick. It's rare, and it's pure poetry.

I believe I nailed four Seamless Flicks on this particular Sunday. That's unheard of. Sunday was a Tour de Flickin' Force. In four hours, I watched the end of the Raiders-Cardinals game, *NFL Primetime*, *The Simpsons*, *Malcolm in the Middle*, a good chunk of *60 Minutes*, enough of the *Brian's Song* remake to know I liked the original better, every play of the Niners-Bills game, and a full-length feature film. Plus, I bathed the kids, read them a story and put them to bed.

I am God.

Here's a brief synopsis of the play-by-play, or flick-by-flick highlights:

7:28 p.m.

Dilemma: After watching racial-profiling story on *60 Minutes* (my token effort at being informed), had planned to bathe kids and move TV so I could watch *NFL Primetime* over shoulder from upstairs bathroom. Simple. But Raiders-Cardinals game is in OT. Will need remote. Difficult to flick properly and watch both kids. Quick adjustment: strip naked, leap into bath, assume position against back wall with both kids and TV now directly in front. Wrap towel around hand and remote to prevent slippage. Smooth work on recall button catches Raiders fumble, Cardinals winning field goal and all early *Primetime* highlights. Other hand cleanses children with rubber ducky sponge. Brilliant.

8:06 p.m.

Another gruelling half-hour. Second half of *Primetime* runs concurrently with *Simpsons*. Wife takes diaper and pajama duty. Team player. **Flick.** Monty Burns has a girlfriend. **Flick.** Rocket Ismail just burned Champ Bailey. **Flick.** I think Monty's about to get nookie. **Flick.** "He... could... go... all... the... way! **Flick.** He did! *Eeeeexcellent, Smithers.*

8:42 p.m.

The Niners game is just starting. Now, usually, a Niners game is a flick-free zone. It's somewhat sacrilegious to browse on your favourite team. But *Malcolm in the Middle* rules. And it's only the Bills. **Flick.** Malcolm, Reese and Dewey are running a black market on stuff donated to their church. **Flick.** Garrison Heart is running, and running, and running. **Flick.** Dewey freakin' kills me. **Flick.** *Brian's Song.* Can't start crying now. **Flick.** The Bills should start crying any minute.

9:13 p.m.

I should be able to coast home from here. There's nothing else I usually watch now except the game. Yet, it's already 14-bagel, and I find my thumb wandering. What's this? Angelina Jolie. Hmmm, *The Bone Collector.* I'm a sucker for mammoth-lipped women in lame serial killer movies. Must return shortly. **Flick.** Ahmed Plummer picks off Alex Van Pelt, who, by the way, is killing the reputation of all the fine Vans who came before him. Dick Van Dyke, Dick Van Patten, Eddie Van Halen, Mario Van Peebles. Greta Van CNN. This guy doesn't deserve a Van. He is Alex Pelt. Period.

10:27 p.m.

Back and forth it goes (unlike the Bills who don't go forth, just back). **Flick.** This killer locks people in his cab, drives them to some abandoned underground rat-infested hell and leaves them to die. So, all in all, a typical cabby. **Flick.** Jeff Garcia to Terrell Owens, six more. Just give the NFL MVP to both of them. **Flick.** Angelina just shot a rat! Those lips take up half the screen. **Flick.** Terrell Owens's touchdown dance is exactly like the funky number Michael J. Fox does at the dance in *Teen Wolf.* **Flick.** Just as the killer is about to stab poor quadriplegic Denzel Washington, The Giant Lips gives him two bullets in the back. Where have I seen that ending before? Oh yeah, the 912 other lame serial killer movies. **Flick.** I believe Alex Pelt wishes someone would shoot him in the back. It's 35-0.

The credits have rolled, so have the Niners. And I head to bed with Terrell, Angelina, Berman, Dewey, Mr. Burns, Morley Safer and Gale Sayers all dancing together inside my head. I check on my sleeping son, and wish he could have stayed up to witness his Dad's Opus. You see, he, too, has the gift. It's genetic.

The boy is barely two. He has a 10-word vocabulary (12 if you include "Eeeeooooo" and "Boodeedee"... I have no idea). He counts to five like this: "Two, two, two, two, two." He believes the dog can, and should, be driving, and protests loudly when I don't let him.

Yet he has full control of the VCR remote, including rewind, fast forward and pause, for the all-important cookie run. And if there's a slow moment during *Blue's Clues* in the morning, he's on that recall button so fast to get to *Clifford the Big Red Dog*, it's scary.

They just make you so proud.

• • •

Postscript: Column was written before the age of the PVR (see "TV Ecstasy", page 147), which has turned Remote Control Flicking into a dying art. It's a shame—this was my one tangible skill I hoped to pass down to future generations. Oh, and by the way, Malcolm in the Middle *really did rule. I'm not sure how it holds up a decade later in syndicated reruns, but back in the day, Frankie Muniz was a comedic genius. Don't ever forget that.*

OVECHKIN:
THE ROCK STAR

September 2008

Washington, DC—The lights are brought down in the concert hall, and the fans go nuts. When the band struts onto the stage, they go nuttier. This is, after all, the hottest act around.

A spotlight finds the lead singer, who is glammed to the max. He wears more eyeliner than Amy Winehouse, and his wild hair is gelled together in one giant spike, like Alfalfa from *The Little Rascals*... on steroids.

He steps to the mic and screams: "Hello DC! Are you ready to rock!?!"

By the ear-drum-blowing response, it's safe to say DC is ready to rock.

The singer smiles his familiar wide, toothy grin. He owns this crowd, even though he can't sing a lick. They don't care. Neither does he.

As the first guitar chord is struck, Alexander Ovechkin grabs the mic stand like it's a hockey stick, scissor-kicks in the air, and starts belting out a song, gleefully oblivious to the fact he barely knows any lyrics and is eons off-key.

No, this is not the strange dream of some Washington Capitals groupie who fell asleep with her iPod on. This is real. Or surreal, anyway.

The Capitals marketing people created the scene themselves. They are filming it for the pre-game opening they'll show on their giant video screen before every home game. Ovechkin is backed up by teammates/guitarists Jose Theodore, Brooks Laich, Alexander Semin, Nik Backstrom and Mike Green (on drums). Donald Brashear and Matt Bradley play the intimidating bodyguards (quite well, I might add). Hundreds of Capitals season-ticket holders act as extras, playing a role that is hardly a stretch: "screaming crowd."

It is a brilliant, and oh-so-appropriate theme, for "Ovie and the Caps" are like a hot young band, poised to make some serious noise in the NHL's Eastern Conference. And the lead singer is the closest thing to a Rock Star that hockey has ever seen.

"He is a Rock Star," says Theodore, the Capitals' new goaltender (and a pretty solid lead guitar player, I might add). "I've never seen anything like it. He has this aura about him. Every time he walks in a building, people just freeze. They are in awe."

"This is just an ordinary day for Alex," says Laich, surveying the scene during a break in filming. "He's a wild man. He's eccentric. He'll try anything. And everybody loves him." It's different, this love. We have always admired our hockey players for their quiet, under-stated demeanor. From Howe to Gretzky to Crosby, the unwritten code of the superstar has always been to leave the flash, the personality on the ice (much to Sean Avery's chagrin).

Well, somebody forgot to tell Ovechkin.

As I watch him prance around the stage, striking every hilarious Whitesnake video pose he can come up with, I try to imagine Crosby or Iginla or Brodeur—or any prominent NHLer—agreeing to do this. No shot. (That's not a knock on them. Wouldn't catch me up there either without a potentially lethal dose of tequila.)

Ovechkin just doesn't care.

"I like having fun," he says later during a break backstage. "That's what life is about, right?"

This may explain why he has, during his brief NHL career: competed on a bizarre Russian game show dressed as a shark (and later, a wolf), begged for dates on another Russian program by giving out his phone number, and accepted the key to the city in Washington, declaring to the crowd: "I'm the president for one day, so everybody have fun and no speed limit!"

And somehow, he finds a way to pull this off without a hint of pretension.

Maybe it is because he doesn't crave attention, like... say... Avery. It craves him. So he just shrugs, and rolls with it.

"Sure, he has that Rock Star aura, but he is a teammate first," says Capitals owner Ted Leonsis. "How many guys would be given a day off by the coach, and drive to Philadelphia on their own to watch the team play a pre-season game? That's why they (his teammates) all embrace him, no matter how much attention he gets."

There was some truth in Avery's comments this week about NHL marketing (despite the tired, self-serving agenda of the mouth they came from). The league needs its players to show more personality. In this 23-year-old Russian goal-scoring machine, it has stumbled upon a potential gold mine.

After the "concert," Ovechkin sits in a stairwell at the back of the theatre, weighing his career options.

"I can dance, I like to shake my popa zhopa," he says with a smile (though I did not major in linguistics, I believe that is Russian slang for "booty").

"But I prefer hockey star to rock star," he smiles. "I don't want to be that famous."

Sorry, son. At this rate, you may not have a choice.

• • •

Postscript: *The video made that night was shown before every Capitals home game that season. It was appropriate. The Capitals finished 50-24-8, their best record in 23 seasons. Ovechkin scored 56 goals and won his second* *straight Hart Trophy. At a Montreal nightclub during All-Star weekend that year, Ovechkin danced on a couch in a private area above the dance floor, while a hundred star-struck young women screamed his name. Apparently, that whole Rock Star video wasn't really a fantasy after all.*

WHO NEEDS GOLF
LESSONS?

September 2000

> *"Easy game, this golf."*
> —Roy McIvoy, *Tin Cup*

Bite me, Roy. It ain't easy. We never believed you, anyway. Though when it comes to fictional movie-golfers, your alter-ego was much better than Matt Damon in *The Legend of Bagger Vance* (when it comes to golf, Mr. Ripley is not so talented).

But I digress. The thing is, my golf game is actually a lot like that other Costner movie. *Waterworld*.

I've killed more fish than Captain High Liner. I've damaged so many trees, environmentalists have chained themselves to the fern in my front yard, demanding I take up bowling. But this year is going to be different. I'm getting help. The other night, I was watching The Shopping Channel when I realized... It was actually The Golf Channel! Easy mistake. I'm sure the "Tony Little 60-Degree Ab-Wedge" cannot be far away.

Man, they have everything you need on there. Slices, Hooks, Shanks, Yips... there are products to cure all of 'em. I grabbed my Visa and ordered a whole bunch of gizmos, each guaranteed to "shave several strokes off my game!" I added up all the stroke-saving, and now expect to shoot a season-opening round of 23.

And so, in the fine tradition of *Consumer Reports*, we review some of the actual products for you.

THE SWING CHECK MIRROR ($29.95)
Description: A round convex mirror that a player places on the ground to get a full view of his or her swing.
Testimonials:
"A great way to check your form before every swing." Julie Smith, California
"It helped me notice the embarrassing grass stains on my ass." James Duthie

THE ON-LINE PUTTING TRAINER ($29.95)
Description: Triangular stakes you stick in the ground in front of your ball to putt through, guaranteeing your putt will stay on-line.
Testimonials:
"I one-putt all the time now!" Jerry Shaw, New Jersey
"It's great! I can now kick my Nana's butt at croquet!" James Duthie

GREG NORMAN'S SECRET ($49.95)
Description: A plastic black splint that fits over the right hand and attaches to the index finger with straps. Designed to maintain proper wrist angle on backswing.
Testimonials:
"If it didn't work, I'd never put my name on it." Greg Norman
"It helped me play just like Norman! I blew a six-stroke lead on the back nine and lost 50 bucks!" James Duthie

THE SWING MATE SPEED METER ($119.95)
Description: Small device that uses radar technology to measure speed of club as it passes by.

Testimonial:
"There's no way I was swinging that fast, officer. And no, I won't take a breathalizer." James Duthie

THE MEDICUS 2000 (4 easy payments of $37.49)
Description: Hinged club that breaks in half when you swing too fast or off-line.
Testimonial: "If I want my club to snap, I'll use a tree." James Duthie

THE SWING JACKET ($133.95)
Description: A flak-jacket type gizmo with arm cuffs that slide along "scientifically positioned rails" guiding you through the perfect golf motion.
Testimonials:
"It's the Ultimate Swing Teacher. I use it." Peter Jacobsen
"The most unrealistic part of the movie *Tin Cup* was that Peter Jacobsen won the US Open." James Duthie

THE POWER SWING FAN ($47.95)
Description: A stick with "fins" at the end, designed to help strengthen your swing and improve distance and accuracy.
Testimonials:
"Within 2–3 weeks, you'll be hitting longer, straighter shots." Dr. Gary Wiren, Master Teaching Professional
"I raked my entire yard with it in less than an hour!" James Duthie

THE SPOT LINER ($8.25)
Description: Little plastic ball cover that helps you draw a perfect X on your ball.
Testimonials: "It's like having a caddie line you up for every putt!" Sheila Code, Tampa
"Here's another letter for you: Y?" James Duthie

THE WONDER STICK ($54.00)
Description: A fibreglass shaft you stick under your left arm and attach to your right forearm to create a perfect swing plane.

Testimonial:
"When I told my wife I'd bought her a Wonder Stick, I'd never seen her so excited!" James Duthie

THE PERFECT LIE ($39.95)
Description: Little piece of fake turf to hit balls off of.
Testimonials:
"It gives me golf course lies in my basement." Al Smith, Los Angeles
"You want a perfect lie? Ask me my score yesterday." James Duthie

Order any of these products and receive my own 100% money-back guaranteed foolproof way to shave dozens of strokes off your game!

Quit after 12 holes when you run out of balls.

• • •

Postscript: Last year, a golfing buddy gave me one of the bracelets that is supposed to help with your balance. I still shoot 93, but I rarely fall down now.

CHELIOS STILL PLAYING? HOW? HOWE!

January 2008

This is how we see Chris Chelios:

Chris Chelios is old!

His name is Greek for Julio Franco. He is the second oldest player in NHL history. Forty-five years, 352 days. He's so old, he makes dirt seem young.

He is older than Sidney Crosby, John Tavares and my eight-year-old son. Combined.

He is older than seven NHL coaches (Babcock, Laviolette, Maurice, Stevens, Sutter, Therrien, Trotz) and eight general managers (Chiarelli, Giguere, Hull, Shero, Snow, Feaster, Ferguson, Nonis).

Scott Niedermayer could retire and un-retire for 11 more seasons, and still be younger than Chelios is now.

He's so old, he has a pin-up of Betty White in his locker.

But wait. Maybe this is how we should see Chris Chelios:

Chris Chelios is young!

He is six years younger than Gordie Howe was when he retired.

His body is 25 years younger. He's a pimple-faced teenage punk compared to Howe at 52. He could play 600 more games, win three more cups and get two more NHLPA directors fired before he catches Gordie.

And silly as it sounds, he might just try.

"It is possible," Chelios says. "I'm not thinking about retiring, that's for sure."

Chelios doesn't like talking about Howe's record much. You get a lot of "We'll see," and "I'm taking it year by year." But the person who knows his physical limits (or lack thereof) better than anyone, believes it isn't just possible, it's probable.

"I truly believe Chelly wants to pass Howe and he will," says TR Goodman, Chelios's off-season trainer for the past 15 summers. "I believe he could play well into his fifties. In fact, I know he can."

Goodman is a former college hockey player who has become a fitness guru for NHL players. And in all his years in the gym in Venice Beach, California, he has never seen a specimen like Chris Chelios.

"He's like a junkyard dog. I'll put the son of a bitch up against any 18-year-old. No one is smarter. No one is in better shape."

And no one is more competitive.

"When I first started training him, the workout would start at 7 a.m., so I would always get there at 6:45 just to be ready," says Goodman. "Then a couple of days into it, I would get there at 6:45 and he would already be there, so I started coming at 6:40. And the next day, he was already there. This kept going until we were getting there at 6 a.m., so I finally said, 'Chelly, would you rather work out earlier?' And he said, very seriously, 'No, I just don't like you beating me to the gym.'"

That story is either cute or disturbing. I'm still trying to decide.

When word of Goodman's workouts started to spread, LA defenseman Rob Blake was one of the first to sign up. He would win the Norris Trophy the year after his first summer training with Goodman. TR's other client wasn't pleased.

"Chelly was so pissed that I'd worked with Rob, he didn't come the next summer and he wouldn't talk to me for a whole year," Goodman says. "He thought I'd taken away his competitive edge by working with Blake."

Chelly did come back. And he hasn't left. The workouts are legendary: six days a week, all summer long. They include one hour straight of doing as many as 16 different exercises over and over without any break. I mean none. No 30-second rests between sets. No chats with the hot girl at the water-cooler. Nada.

By comparison, I often nap between sets of push-ups.

And when Chelios leaves the gym, he usually relaxes with a three-hour mountain bike ride followed by a couple of hours of paddling a surfboard on the ocean. At some point, it's believed he sits down to eat. Slacker.

"I will tell you this," Chelios says. "When I do retire, it won't be because of motivation. Something physical would have to happen to stop me from playing."

He means an injury. Not age.

Still, 52?!? Chelios would not pass Howe's record until Feb. 1, 2014.

Most of the players I spoke to placed his chances of making it at somewhere between none and... noner.

"Ten years ago, no one was working out like Chelly, but now a lot of guys train like that," says one. "It doesn't give him the advantage it used to. It's amazing what he's doing. But six more years? No shot."

Congrats. You've just provided this junkyard dog with more bulletin board material to try to prove you wrong.

"What people don't understand is that Chelly is actually in better shape now than he was a few years ago," says Goodman. "He doesn't do all that running he used to so his knees are way better. People talk about Gordie Howe, but I think the man who inspires Chelly now is Don Wildman, the guy who founded Bally's Fitness. He rides with Chelly, and I think Don has shown him he has the potential to be an elite athlete for a very long time."

Don Wildman, by the way, is 72.

• • •

Postscript: *That season, Chelios went on to win his third Stanley Cup ring with Detroit. The following season he played just 28 games with the Red Wings, a healthy scratch most nights. He played most of the 2009-2010 season with the Chicago Wolves of the American Hockey League before being signed by the Atlanta Thrashers, where he played just seven games. It was likely the quiet end to a remarkable 28-year pro career. I say "likely" because I won't believe Chris Chelios is really retired until he's...oh...93. And even then, he'll still beat you to the gym.*

MY SPORTS SABBATICAL

August 2002

"I know you're in there!" she yells, pounding on the bathroom door. "And I know you've got the Sports section!"

Uh-Oh. Nabbed. It was eerily reminiscent of the scene in *Traffic* when Michael Douglas catches his daughter getting high in her bathroom, all panicky and loopy-eyed.

Yup, that was me. Doing my best Erika Christensen... getting my fix off a couple of boxscores. I could have tried to flush it... but it was *The Sun*. Too thick. So I was done. Beaten. Looking back now, I believe it was a cry for help.

• • •

Earlier that summer...

It was just one of those goofy nonsensical things we males say after a couple of beverages on a summer vacation night. Kind of like: "Let's drive to South Carolina right now!" Or: "I could do that Hawaii Triathlon if I trained a couple months." And the always popular: "If J-Lo got to know me, I'd have a shot."

After spending four perfect cottage days on the couch, watching roughly 22 and a half hours a day of the British Open, I made an off-the-cuff pledge to my wife.

"OK. No more following sports for the rest of my vacation."

I meant it, too. No watching games. No *SportsCenter*. No All-Sports Radio. No browsing Kournikova websites (thus ignoring 47 of 49 bookmarks).

I was going cold turkey. A holiday from Halladay. A Sabbatical from Sabathia. An Olerud Interlude. My own personal All-Star break.

Now, I'm no chimp. You don't make that vow in the fall. Or winter or spring, for that matter. There's too much to miss. But this was summer. These were the dog days.

It's not like I'd break into a cold sweat over skipping that Braves-D-Rays series on TBS. Or the Comets-Monarchs showdown on the WNBA Game-of-the-Week. When the World Professional Chuckwagon Tour tops the Sunday afternoon schedule, I believe it's a safe time to escape.

Sure, I'd miss a few CFL games and a free-agent signing or two, but heck, I could catch up. Plus, it would be good for me. A self-cleansing. A rediscovery of the joy and wonder of life away from this pathetic existence of endless scores and hilites.

And it worked. I was like the bubble boy on his first day without the bubble.

It's amazing. Without games to watch, and *SI* issues to read, and *Golf Academy Live* to mess with your backswing, you suddenly have time to get reacquainted with the rest of your life.

Among my revelations:

- We still have a dog? (I swore he ran away right after the second kid arrived.)

- Holy crap, we have a second kid!

- *Dawson's Creek* is still on!?! What are they now, 40? I believe the episode I watched had Katie Holmes coping with the early stages of menopause.

Oh, the things I'd been missing. Suddenly, I had time for conversations with my wife that actually went beyond:

"Just two more minutes honey... they're only down three!"

We went for long walks in the woods. OK the mall, but same diff.

I actually read books by someone other than John Feinstein. The kids starting calling me "Daddy" instead of "Mommy's funny-looking friend who lives on the couch."

I was reborn!

• • •

It lasted three days.

OK, two and change. I relapsed more often than Robert Downey Jr. I'd take anything. Faking work in the basement to watch a playoff in the LPGA's Big Apple Classic. Pretending to browse the Net for pre-school education information while actually prepping my fantasy football draft. Sick.

It ended with that whole *Traffic* bathroom scene. She just laughed at me. That horrifying "I know you better than you know yourself" laugh that only a spouse can do. Defeated and deflated, the hopeless addict sulked back downstairs.

Just in time.

For the Niners and Skins from Japan, baby!

• • •

Postscript: *That was a really stupid idea. Don't ever try it.*

PLEASE RELEASE ME

February 2005. (NHL lockout year)

This is a Dear John letter.

As in Leclair, Madden, Grahame, etc.

It's also a Dear Jon letter (Klemm), a Dear John Michael letter (Liles) and a Dear Joni letter (Pitkanen). You get the idea.

The point is, I'm done with you guys. We're breaking up. Oh, and don't think this is just an anti-player rant. I'm done with Bettman and his boys, too. I'm neutrally bitter.

You see, I used to host hockey games. Now I host mind games.

Let's see. We started doing regular lockout panel chats in September. So... roughly five a week... two a day since January... sometimes three... carry the one... dang, I wish I'd paid attention in math... must use computer calculator instead... equals... somewhere around 150 lockout discussions. Or about 147 more than Gary and Bob have had over the same period.

I'm dizzy from the rhetoric. I feel like I've been on a four-day bender with Nick Nolte. And for what? I feel the same way I did after I saw *Lost in Translation*: You mean, that's it? What the hell did it mean? (Though I'll take Scarlett Johansson over Daly and Saskin.)

We've all been held hostage by these guys. And trust me, there is no chance of Stockholm Syndrome. So, as soon as the smoke clears on D-Day, I'm out.

You will not read another word about the NHL in this column.

(Of course, when you've written two columns in the last six months, one about football and one about baseball, this isn't exactly standing in front of the tank in Tiananmen Square. But play along. Let me feel like a badass for once in my life.)

I will write a 10,000-word thesis entitled "Ribbon: The Misunderstood Element of Rhythmic Gymnastics" before I write another NHL column.

I will cover the 2005 Regional Seniors' Cribbage Qualifier in Tweed before I type another word about the No Hockey League.

I will wax poetic about my five-year-old boy's proficiency at magnetic darts before I devote any more space to the... Actually, I might write that column. The kid's got a gift. Triple 20s by the handful. I'm going to start taking him to pubs to play drunk guys for money.

We are over, the NHL and I. We are so Brad and Jen.

Oh, I'll come back someday. I love the game too much not to. Plus, there is that tiny detail about being paid to host games. But until then, this is it. I'm going back to essays about Elin Nordegren's navel.

Of course, you will get stuck with me for endless hours of pre- and post-apocalyptic coverage on TSN for the next few days. Thus, as my final contribution to this ridiculous, infuriating process, I give you the following easy-reference guide to help you fully comprehend the lockout-lingo you will be hearing.

Significant Philosophical Differences: Gary hates Bob. Bob hates Gary.

Cost Certainty: A guarantee that the price you pay for Leafs tickets will continue to rise under a salary cap.

Impasse and Implementation: When you argue with your wife over the logic of buying $2,000 imported drapes, and then come home from work the next day to find she's already had them installed. Sorry. I have some scars.

24% Rollback: When you have dinner with TSN football analyst Chris Schultz and he asks for a tiny bite of your dinner roll, this is what you get.

Revenue Sharing: When a sizable portion of your pay cheque goes to the guy who installs the imported drapes. Deep scars.

Hard Cap: What Bettman and Goodenow better wear in any public place where there may be hockey fans carrying projectiles.

Triggers: The part of the gun you'll use to shoot yourself if you have to sit through any more of this crap.

• • •

Postscript: I kept my word. Sort of. I didn't write another column until a month into the post-lockout NHL. I would have held out longer, except for this minor detail about needing to be paid.

NO DOUBTING THOMAS

January 2009

For my money, the most entertaining player in hockey isn't Ovechkin or Malkin. It's a guy who has never scored a goal, and often resembles a freshly caught fish on the bottom of a boat.

Boston's Tim Thomas is the best thing to happen to goaltending since the mask.

Where do I start? He's small, so his equipment doesn't make him eclipse the net like some of those Jabba the Hutt look-alikes. He doesn't have one of those robotic techniques. Heck, I'm not sure he has any technique! If he does the butterfly, it looks like it's missing a wing, flying in all directions. Every night with Thomas is like Live at the Improv. He's made the position fun again.

"Do you want to look pretty getting scored on, or ugly making the save?" he asks with a rhetorical chuckle.

Thomas makes ugly, ridiculous, impossible saves nightly.

And just to make things interesting, he's occasionally awful. When that happens, when he flips when he should have flopped, he gets so mad at himself, it looks like David Banner turning into The Hulk.

"With most goalies, you know their tendencies, but Timmy doesn't have any tendencies," says Tampa Bay forward Martin St. Louis, who played with Thomas at the University of Vermont. "I have a tougher time scoring against him than almost any other goalie."

Good or bad (and the latter is becoming increasingly rare), Thomas is never dull. My buddy, a diehard Bruins fan, calls him "terrifying to watch." (And he wears a Thomas jersey.)

And he almost never got to watch him. For his entire hockey playing life, Thomas was told he had zero shot at making the NHL. Which is probably the exact reason he did.

He grew up in Flint, Michigan, around the time Michael Moore made *Roger and Me*, a movie about the town dying. His Dad, Tim Sr., was a used car salesman at a time when no one in Flint could afford a car. So he sold apples door-to-door. He'd sell 10 bushels, use some of the money to buy seven more, and give those to Tim to sell. That's how Jr. raised his money to play hockey.

When things got really bad, his parents pawned their wedding rings to pay for Tim to go to a goalie school.

The son didn't find out until his Dad bought his Mom a new one many years later.

He wore the same beaten-up pads for years, repairing them over and over until they... well... disintegrated.

"I was playing for the Lakeland Jets and (former NHLer) Joe Murphy was skating with us while he was holding out with the Oilers," Thomas says. "He took a shot and it literally went right through my pad and out the backside."

Murphy would do more for the young goalie than give him a great story for beer-night. Thomas was a never-see-the-ice third-stringer on that Lakeland junior team, so he started playing forward. But right after the Christmas break, the starting goalie missed his flight back from Alaska and the backup got in a car accident. So Thomas took all the shots in practice. As he was skating off the ice, he heard Murphy say to the coach: "Why aren't you playing that guy?"

So he did. Every game for the rest of the year. That launched Thomas on a netminding odyssey that would take him to, in chronological order: Vermont (University), Helsinki, Birmingham (ECHL),

Houston (IHL), Hamilton (AHL), Helsinki (again), Detroit (IHL), Sweden, back to Finland, Providence (AHL), Boston (cup of coffee), Providence, Helsinki (this is getting silly), Providence, and, finally, at the age of 32, Boston... to stay.

"It never once crossed my mind to quit," Thomas says. "But at one point, I did make peace with the fact I'd be playing in Europe for the rest of my career."

He might have, except that when a bunch of other NHL goalies came over to Europe during the lockout, Thomas outplayed them all, and forced the Bruins to take another look. Three years later, they're still looking.

His competitiveness is legendary. As a junior, he was invited to the US Olympic Festival, essentially a tryout camp for the World Juniors. The players were split into four squads and played a round-robin. Thomas played half of each of the four games, and gave up just one goal as his team won the tournament. The other goalie on his squad gave up 11, and he was the one picked for the World Junior team.

"I was so mad," recalls Thomas. "USA Hockey had bought me a dozen sticks, and it was the first time anyone had bought me sticks, so it was huge for me. Well, I went in the back room and demolished every stick against the wall. I was irate."

Even better story: when he played at Vermont, he once got so mad after being scored on, he picked up the puck and launched it at the scoreboard, shattering lights and causing a fireworks show reminiscent of Roy Hobbs's last home run in *The Natural*. And that was in practice.

"There were pieces of light falling over the ice," says St. Louis, chuckling. "It was hilarious."

Just watch Thomas when he loses a shootout. He sprints off the ice like someone tossed a grenade in his net. Like they're going to send him back to Flint to sell apples.

Somewhat sadly, we're not seeing many of those Thomas tantrums anymore (Angry Tim is my favourite Tim). He just doesn't get scored on much. He was an All-Star last year and his .944 save percentage leads the NHL this season.

And yet, so typical of his Dangerfield existence, he was left off the All-Star ballot. There they go. Doubting Thomas. Again.

"I'm going to have to disappoint you and give you a 'No comment' on that one," he says. That's OK. Sometimes "No comment" says more than a dozen quoted paragraphs.

The ballot snub is just more motivation to go out and contort his body into all those bizarre, wonderful shapes that somehow keep pucks on the happy side of the goal line.

"Dominik Hasek on steroids," as one opposing forward puts it.

And with every save, every win, it's as if Thomas is speaking to all of those who doubted him along the way, saying:

"How do you like them apples?"

• • •

Postscript: Thomas would go on to win the Vezina Trophy that season, as the NHL's best goaltender. In his acceptance speech, he talked about his parents and everything he had overcome. Then he broke down in tears.

RISE OF THE RAVEN

March 2003

A magical era ended last weekend.

My beloved alma mater, Carleton U, saw its unparalleled and unprecedented run of never winning... anything... ever... come to a stunning end with a CIS Men's Basketball Championship in Halifax. In the aftermath, I was overwhelmed with emotion.

I mean, WHAT THE HECK WERE THEY THINKING!?! Decades spent perfecting futility, and they throw it all away?!? Talk about disrespecting your alumni.

You see, in my day, we liked losing. Losing was what set Carleton apart. It was our *thang*.

Saskatchewan and Saint Mary's had football. Manitoba, volleyball. Brandon, hoops. Schools like UBC, Alberta, Western, McGill... they were good at almost everything.

And Carleton? Hmmm. Well, we had a relatively solid fencing program, from what I remember. Sabre especially. Épée, not so much. Besides that, we bit.

During the late '80s, CU's policy of admitting almost everyone who applied (a friend of mine still claims he got in with three Grade 13 credits and a 47 percent average) got the school dubbed "Last Chance U." But when it came to sports, we were "No Chance U."

The only sporting event people at Carleton got excited about was the annual Panda Game against Ottawa U. We even won that sometimes. But it hardly mattered. Most spent the day cheering for the water balloons slung-shot from the Carleton side of Frank Clair Stadium to the Ottawa U side (we were good at that—solid engineering program at Carleton).

Smacking Ottawa U students with balloons and chanting "What the *#%@'s a Gee-Gee!?!" were pretty much all that mattered.

The football team was actually good. Once. They made the Churchill Bowl my freshman year (1986). And lost 50-10. Two years later, they were 0-7, and then 0-7 again, starting a downslide that would eventually lead to the program being killed in 1998. The reaction on campus was shock:

"You've got to be kidding! We had a football team?"

But it wasn't just football. We sucked at everything. Except sucking back. A study once revealed Carleton students drank more beer per capita than any other university. And that was *during* class.

Oh, we knew sports at CU. We just couldn't play them. In my journalism class alone, the graduates included Jason Kay, editor of *The Hockey News*; Rand Simon, a key man in agent Don Meehan's company; Ken Warren, hockey writer for the *Ottawa Citizen*; and David Naylor, sportswriter for *The Globe and Mail*. We would have kicked ass if there were an all-sports *Reach For The Top*.

The great Homer Simpson once said there's only two kinds of people at college: "jocks and nerds." We were a little nerd heavy (hence, my presence).

While other schools were known for their particular sporting prowess, when you told people you went to Carleton, you'd get:

"Carleton eh? You guys got a great... Architecture Program."

Darn tootin' we do! We could draw up a killer shopping mall, just not a zone defense.

And that's why I loved Carleton. We didn't have to bother battling for bragging rights every year. We didn't care. There was no attitude, like certain other schools which I won't name.

OK, Queen's and Western.

But now, look what's happened! The basketball team wins the title. The men's soccer team comes second, losing the national final in OT. Women's soccer finishes top 10, the swim teams make the nationals for only the second time ever, and both the men's and women's Nordic ski teams win their nationals.

Suddenly, The Ravens are a powerhouse. OK, that's a stretch.

But they're respectable. Twelfth overall in the National Sports Power Rankings.

In my day, I believe we were 178th, just behind Moosejaw Community College.

And it's not just sports. The former "Last Chance U" is now rated in the top 10 schools overall in the annual *Maclean's* survey.

It's just wrong. I long for the old Raven-way, those not-so glory days, when we were so bad, I could actually pass for a jock.

• • •

Postscript: *The Ravens basketball team is now one of the greatest dynasties in Canadian university history, winning championships six out of eight years, as of 2010. Alumni from my era continue to bow our heads in shame.*

RIVAL ETERNAL

December 2005

The romantics say we all have a soul mate out there somewhere. (And for the last time, Charlize Theron, I'm not yours, so please stop calling.)

Maybe. But this I know for sure: we do have a sport mate, a half best buddy/half nemesis we are destined to compete with for forever. The French use the term *rivalle eternalle*. Eternal rival. (Clearly, I made that up. The French don't call it anything. I just was trying to sound worldly again.)

Ali had Frazier. Magic had Larry. Sidney has Ovie. And I have Mark Ward.

I met Wardo in Grade 3, when we invented a bizarre hybrid of soccer, hockey and basketball, where you try to kick a rubber puck between the two base-posts of the playground basketball hoop to score. It was pure genius (we're still bitter we don't get the props Naismith gets), and occupied every winter recess of our public school existence.

The problem was Wardo happened to be better than me at Sock-eyehoop. He was a sick combination of Beckham, Jagr and LeBron (in a 3-foot-10 kid-in-snow-boots kind of way).

And this drove me nuts.

Even worse, he could climb the steep aluminum slope and get on the roof of our school, which, in summertime, was carpeted with brand new tennis balls sprayed by adults who practised against the school wall. This made him God of Glen Ogilvie Public. Fresh Slazengers were like crack to Grade 3 boys. Not for tennis, but for road hockey, baseball, Chance (throw ball against wall, must catch it on the way back or you're out). Tennis balls were currency. And he was Bill flippin' Gates.

I would try to climb up for hours, and couldn't get half way. So I'd sit on the grass and catch all the balls he'd throw down. Reduced to a ball boy at age eight. Sad.

This is my first memory of competitive fire. And the moment a lifelong rivalry was born. Wardo would become my best friend. And my eternal rival. My Newman.

For the next 20 years, we would compete at everything. Running, jumping, climbing, marbles, baseball, soccer, hockey, football, basketball, tennis, badminton, wrestling, golf, mini-golf, dodgeball, lawn darts, Frogger, flexed arm-hang, Toss-A-Cross, Risk, hockey-card flipping, Crazy 8s, Electronic Quarterback, caps and, eventually… girls.

And that doesn't even take into account the zillions of games we invented. You don't understand. This went on every waking moment we were together. Waiting for the school bus? Who can hit the stop sign with the snowball first! Bored in class? Who can peg Darryl Fogel in the head with a piece of eraser!

We used to walk two miles to the local mini-golf (racing at the end), play three rounds like it was the fifth major, hit two buckets of balls (with an intricate points system for hitting various targets), then wager on how many cars would pass before my Mom picked us up.

It was a two-kid daily decathlon.

We once invented a two-man game of baseball we played on our knees in my basement using one of my Dad's drumsticks for a bat, and a ping-pong ball. We started this when we were 10. It ended only when I moved from that house.

At 21.

This rivalry continued well into our 30s, and it went beyond sport.

Just before I moved to Vancouver in 1997, we went on one last boy's road trip to Newfoundland. One night at a bar on George Street, we were talking to a cute blonde. When she excused herself to go to the washroom, Wardo said: "She's totally into me."

"Yeah, right." I said.

"She's just being friendly, moron. It's Newfoundland. They're friendly to everyone."

So, of course, it was game on. I stayed in the same spot. Wardo moved to the other side of the mostly empty bar. If she came out, and went to him, he'd win.

Well, she comes out, starts towards me, notices Wardo isn't there, and beelines across the bar to him. He did a victory dance Chad Johnson would be envious of. And just to flaunt his win, he married her.

When my wife gave birth to our first, my first call was to Wardo. It was a touching moment between two lifelong friends.

"One-nothing sucker! I am kicking your ass in babies!"

It went back and forth from there. For the record, it's now 3-3, and due to... umm... procedures... is destined to end that way. Though I'm pondering adopting a baby from China, just to beat him.

Wardo lives in Newfoundland now, so the games have been reduced to hockey pools and one golf weekend a year. But the new generation brings hope.

Last year, a bunch of old friends got together for an afternoon at a park in Ottawa. Wardo was in town with his oldest son (age four), and I brought mine (age 4.5).

We raced them.

For the record, my boy crushed Wardo's boy by 10 feet. We totally rule.

(*By the way, if this constitutes some form of abuse, please don't contact authorities.)

(**Unless you are in Newfoundland. If they take Wardo's kid away, I'll lead 3-2 again.)

• • •

Postscript: *Wardo and I played golf together last summer. I had him by a stroke or two all day, until he tied me on 17. Then on 18, he hit an impossible Bob Twayish bunker shot to beat me by one. I hate that guy. But I got even. Wardo actually wrote his own column in response to this, to prove he could write better than me, too. It was pretty good. He wanted me to put it in the book, but then he would have been a published author, too. I couldn't allow that. So I cut it. I now lead him 1-0 in hardcover publishing. Sucka!*

THE LONGEST SEASON

April 2010

The phone rang around 2:30 in the morning.

One of those disorienting, middle-of-the-night calls, when you grab the phone before you know where you are, before you know whether you are awake or dreaming. It had to be the latter. The words coming from the other end of the line made no sense.

"What?!? How?!? No!"

Taylor Pyatt dropped the phone.

• • •

It is springtime in Canada, when we inevitably lose our minds about hockey, and talk about wins and losses as if they are life and death. They are, of course, nothing remotely close. And no one knows this better than Pyatt, a tall, bruising forward for the Phoenix Coyotes.

A little over a year ago, he was getting ready for a play-off run with the Vancouver Canucks, and a summer wedding to his long-time girlfriend, Carly Bragnalo.

"We were together 11 years, high school sweethearts." Pyatt says. "She was just an amazing person. She just...always made me feel comfortable. We had a great relationship."

"Everyone loved her," says Taylor's younger brother Tom, a forward with the Montreal Canadiens. "She was always happy. She loved to cook. She was always cooking up big feasts for us at the cottage."

Their cottage, in Thunder Bay, is where Taylor and Carly were to be married. But on April 2nd, 2009, just four months before the wedding, that phone call in the middle of the night changed...everything.

"We had a game at home that night against Anaheim. I just went home and had something to eat, and went to sleep. I got a call at 2:30am from Carly's brother. I was still half asleep; I didn't know what he was saying. I couldn't comprehend it. I just dropped the phone. Then I got a call about 15 seconds later from her Dad. He said Carly had been killed in a car accident. I couldn't believe it...I kept asking him over and over, 'Are you sure, are you sure?' I was in total shock."

Bragnalo was vacationing in Jamaica. She was in a taxi with her Mom and three others when the driver lost control around a corner, flipped, and hit a utility pole. Carly was the only fatality.

Taylor Pyatt sits in a dressing room at the Coyotes' arena in Glendale, Arizona, squeezing an empty water bottle over and over nervously. This is the first time he has spoken publicly about Carly's death and his year in Hell.

He is a quiet guy at the best of times, so finding the right words is a struggle. You want to tell him you understand. Right words? They don't exist.

"It was just a devastating time for me. I got on a flight and went home right away. I was surrounded by my family for the next few weeks, but I was in total shock. The first few days, making funeral arrangements, making plans to get her back...her body back, all those sort of things you thought you would never do, especially at this point of your life. I remember asking myself, 'Are you really doing this?'"

"It felt like a bad dream," says Tom Pyatt. "I flew right home and Taylor was already there, with friends. There's not much you can say. I just gave him a big hug and told him I'd be there for him."

Taylor would spend the next three weeks in Thunder Bay, trying to figure out why the world had leveled him from behind. Answers never came.

He returned to the Canucks, just before their playoff series with Chicago, hoping to lose himself in hockey. Going to the rink, seeing the guys, trying to win games—it helped.

But once the team was eliminated, he was left alone, to a summer of mourning, with a feeling that he needed to get far, far away.

"I felt it was time to move on from Vancouver, time to turn the page, for my personal life and my career."

Pyatt was a free agent, and in the harsh world of professional hockey, he was now a bit of a risk. He was a 27 year-old budding journeyman (he had played for the Islanders and Buffalo before Vancouver) coming off a so-so season, and he was a mess mentally. Damaged.

Only one general manager called him. Don Maloney of the Phoenix Coyotes.

"We drafted his brother Tom in New York, so I knew the family," say Maloney. "We didn't have the resources to offer him what he'd been making in Vancouver, but I wanted to see how he was doing, and tell him why this would be a great fit for him."

Phoenix was hardly a desired destination for most free agents last summer. The team was in bankruptcy court, ownerless, and hadn't made the playoffs in eight years. It seemed like a one-way ticket to hockey obscurity. And maybe that's what made it the perfect place for Taylor Pyatt.

"He was looking for a fresh start," says Maloney. "I think he looked at us in the desert being as far away from all the attention in Canada as you can imagine."

He was right.

Pyatt did need to get away. Away from everything that reminded him of his old life. Of Carly. So he became a Phoenix Coyote.

Play through pain. That's what hockey players are supposed to do, right? But there was no treatment for this. No ice bags, no pills, no rehab. It was unrelenting. Paralyzing.

"I think early on in the season I struggled quite a bit. It was much harder than I thought. Mentally, emotionally, the ups and downs of hockey can be tough by themselves. But to add on the grieving process...at times it was really difficult. If I had a tough game, in the morning I felt pretty low. I started to wonder if I should step away from the game for a bit...if my heart was still in it."

During those tough first few months, Pyatt became good friends with Keith Yandle, the Coyotes star-in-the-making defenceman. They would hang out, go to dinner, and when Pyatt was ready, talk.

"He's a quiet guy, and I didn't really know what was going on inside him. But once he got comfortable, sometimes he'd want to talk about it, and so I'd just listen. That's all you can do is be there to listen.

"I think it helped him. He started to come out of his shell. He likes to laugh, joke around. It's great to see. I'm engaged right now and I couldn't imagine what happened to him happening to me. He's a really strong kid, and a great guy."

As the season wore on, and the Coyotes started winning, hockey started to matter again to Pyatt.

"It was hard early," says Maloney. "The holidays were really hard for him. He sat out some games when he wasn't as good as he needed to be. But, the last month he's been terrific. When he's focused, he's an unstoppable force."

It's been a year now. And Taylor Pyatt is healing. Slowly.

"There was no one day that I was suddenly ready to move on," says Pyatt. "It just comes and goes, and you learn to live with it. I still struggle every day. I still think about Carly every day. But I'm not as emotional as I was. I can smile and laugh about the good times we had. I love playing hockey, and I'm excited about this team and its chances. I'm looking forward to getting that happiness and joy back in my life."

• • •

Postscript: *Pyatt played inspired hockey down the stretch and in the playoffs for Phoenix, but his Coyotes were eliminated in the first round in seven games by Detroit.*

HOCKEY'S GREAT RECESSION

February 2008

It is hockey's secret crisis. A subject few NHL players want to discuss publicly, but many fret about privately.

They try to hide it. Cover it up. But if they have it, they know that eventually they will be found out.

No, not HGH, silly. MPB! Male Pattern Baldness.

In today's NHL, the feathers are flying faster than the fists.

Twenty-one-year-olds are already looking like Messier. And I'm not talking about their leadership abilities. Many young hockey heads are in the midst of a full-scale recession.

I'm not going to name names. This isn't the *Mitchell Report*. I don't foresee any Congressional Hearings on this matter.

Indiana Congressman Dan Burton: "We have sworn affidavits that you were wearing a ball cap at the team party in the summer of 2006? What were you hiding?

Balding Player: "Uhh… nothing, sir. It was sunny out."

Congressman: "Lies! The party was inside! There was no need for cranial protection! Show us the top of your head, son! Showwww Ussssss!"

Besides, you watch *SportsCenter.* You see the post-game interviews. You can tell which scalps are playing shorthanded.

Sure, a percentage of all young men lose their locks early. But this is an epidemic.

"The numbers [of balding hockey players] must be way above the norm," says player agent JP Barry, himself a proud card-carrying member of the hair-impaired.

"There really are a lot of balding guys in hockey," says Ottawa native Matthew Barnaby, a hair and teeth guy now for TSN and ESPN. "At least most of them now just shave their heads because there were a few guys who got those plugs, and it wasn't pretty."

It could be some freakish statistical anomaly, something hereditary in hockey's collective lineage. Or (cue the *60 Minutes* clock-ticking soundtrack), it could be something more sinister.

After a lengthy in-depth investigation (I made a few calls from my couch while eating Doritos), I have learned that many players believe the cause of their follicle frustrations lies… in their helmets.

"I've definitely heard that complaint in the dressing room," says one NHLer, whose scalp happens to be fully stocked. "We have one third-year guy who has lost a ton just since he came into the league. He was bitching to his equipment rep about the helmets."

The belief is that somehow the foam interior of the helmets, there to protect players from head injuries, is literally rubbing their hair away.

"The issue hasn't been raised with me," says NHL Player Association Executive Director Paul Kelly, who wears his full head of hair in the trendy "Retro-Glen Sather" style. "That's because they either are a little embarrassed to raise such an issue, or believe—as I do—that bald ain't so bad! Maybe we can consider asking the guys to wear full head bubbles like in the movie *Apollo 13* and lay to rest the baldness and visor issue in one swoop."

(This is why I like Paul Kelly. You just didn't get that kind of material from Saskin or Goodenow.)

My extensive research on the subject (one Google search) led me to Dr. Robert M. Bernstein, a clinical professor of dermatology at Columbia University and the founder of the Bernstein Center for

Hair Restoration in New York. He is also a past winner of the "Platinum Follicle Award." The knowledge that this award exists will provide me endless amusement for years to come. The Platinum Follicle Award is the Hart Trophy of the hair-loss world.

I asked Dr. Bernstein about the possibility of hockey helmets causing baldness.

"No chance. There have been rare cases of traction causing hair loss but that does not involve a normal pattern of baldness and it is usually around the temples and sideburn area. If the players have typical male pattern baldness, it is definitely genetic."

Still, Gary Bettman may want to consider hiring Sy Sperling as a special assistant. Something has to be done. Our game may not be able to survive another Al Iafrate balding mullet—the dreaded "Skullet"—or Rob Brown, who seemed to have... how do I put this... a very solid forward line, but no D.

Look, I'm hardly one to mock the coifs of others. After all, my old *CFL on TSN* pal Matt Dunigan used to tell me I looked like I combed my hair with a rock. But if indeed more young players are losing their lids, it is a true tragedy. "Hockey hair" is one of the great traditions of our game.

Where have you gone, Ron Duguay? A (hockey) nation turns its lonely eyes to you. Ooh, ooh, ooh.

There is some historical irony in all of this. In the 1940s, Boston Bruin Johnny Crawford became one of the first players to wear a leather helmet regularly in the NHL. He didn't do it for protection.

He did it to cover up his bald head.

• • •

Postscript: This investigative report was somehow overlooked when they handed out the Pulitzers. Robbed again. Meanwhile, the king of hockey hair, Ron Duguay, did return to the spotlight in 2009, on Battle of the Blades, *a show that pairs figure skaters with ex-hockey players. He lost, but his hair remains formidable. It is a national treasure.*

BIG FISH ON THE
FROZEN POND

June 2008

There is a wonderful scene at the end of *Big Fish*, a movie that makes me bawl like Dick Vermeil, where the son rushes his dying father to a river. When he gets there, the father finds all the people who mattered in his life waiting by the riverbank, applauding. (He then dives into the water and turns into a fish, just so you're clear we're not talking documentary here.)

This is what the NHL Draft reminds me of.

Except unlike Albert Finney's dreamy death scene, Friday night was only the beginning for these gifted 18-year-olds. The draft is really a celebration of the people who helped them get this far.

"Having everyone here to watch is what makes it special," first overall pick Steven Stamkos says. "Your family, your coaches, your friends, I think it's a moment where they all realize the influence they've had on your life. That they've been a big part of your success."

Stamkos had a group of 60 on hand: Mom, Dad, sis, aunts, uncles, cousins, coaches. And, of course, buds: Adam, Justin, Kyle, Mark,

Bobby, another Adam... there were more, but my hand got tired of writing. Stamkos wanted them mentioned, because, he says, it's their day, too. (To say this kid "gets it" is an understatement.)

And he's right. It is their day, too. The seats at Scotiabank Place were full of the main characters in the screenplay of these kids' lives.

Moms and dads who tied skates in the freezing cold for those 5:30 a.m. practices. Older brothers who fired shots in the basement until little bro's body looked like a week-old pear. Younger sisters who had to miss the Hilary Duff concert to go to some tournament in Buffalo. That peewee coach with the funny moustache who kept telling you you'd never make it if you didn't backcheck. And those buddies from grade school who liked you way before you made Bob McKenzie's blog.

There were about 1,300 tickets allotted for families and friends at this draft. There were more than 3,000 requests.

Friday's first round was like one big episode of *Entourage*, except instead of Turtle, Drama and E, it was Grandpa Ernie, Coach Pete and Aunt Mildred.

Second overall pick Drew Doughty had almost 50 in his group, including his grandparents Marie and Edward.

"Our family didn't have a lot of money when I was growing up, so they'd always help pay for things and give me rides. It meant everything to me."

Toronto's blue-chip blueliner Luke Schenn had a group of about 25 cheering him on, including Barry and Ingrid Davidson, his junior hockey billet family in Kelowna.

"They've been like a second set of parents to me. There was no way they were going to miss it," Schenn says.

Cody Hodgson, who went 10th overall to Vancouver, had a slew of past coaches who impacted his life, including Paul Titanic (who had a bunch of first-rounders to clap for), Tyler Cragg and even Jim Winn, who coached him at the impressionable age of... four.

"He taught me to give and go with the puck. I never forgot it," Hodgson says with a smile.

And then there's likely the smallest posse of all. Fifth overall selection Nikita Filatov had only his parents, Helen and Slava, with him from Russia.

"I owe everything to my Mom," Filatov says, in excellent English, which his mother has been teaching him since he was four. "Everything I have accomplished, it is all because of her."

"He is such a good boy," Helen says proudly, eyes moistening. "This is the moment he has worked for all his life." (Aside: Helen also wanted the hockey world to know that Elton John messed up with his song "Nikita." Nikita is not a girl's name in Russia. Boys only. It drives her nuts when she hears the tune. Safe to say Elton is not on any Filatov iPods.)

Alas, not everyone made it to watch his or her Big Fish make the jump. Colin Wilson's roommate Vic from Boston University was going to come. That is, until Colin got locked out of the dorm in his underwear at 5 a.m. Thursday while trying to move some stuff to his car. He had to throw rocks at the window to get let back in. When the alarm went off a couple of hours later, Vic wasn't budging.

"Sorry, dude," he said. "I'll watch it on TV."

• • •

Postscript: The NHL Draft remains my favourite event, every season. The only difficult part is watching kids who expect to go in the first round drop lower. Landon Ferraro, the son of my TSN colleague, former NHL star Ray Ferraro, desperately hoped to be a first-rounder at the 2009 Draft in Montreal. He was sitting just a section up from the stage where we were broadcasting. As name after name was called, I would glance up and see the increasing anxiety painted on his face. When the 30th and last name was called that night, he bolted from the arena in seconds. "That was a really hard night," Ray would tell me later. But the next morning, Ferraro's name was the second one called, 32nd overall by the Detroit Red Wings. All the disappointment of the night before was gone in a heartbeat. "He didn't take off that Red Wings hat for three days," says Ray.

TORTURE TUNNEL

November 2009

I have a new least favourite acronym. Leaping past PMS into top spot: MRI.
You know the term. You hear us use it all the time.

"Sidney Crosby will have an MRI Friday..."

"Chris Bosh still awaiting the results of his MRI..."

"The MRI revealed a tear in his left buttock."

Well, if you don't know what MRI stands for, I'm here to tell you.
It stands for... DEATH TRAP! HELL HOLE! TORTURE CHAMBER!
RUN FOR YOUR LIVES!

Oh sure, the medical community will tell you it stands for "Magnetic Resonance Imaging." Whatever. More like "Most Revolting Incident"... of my adult life. I just had my first, and last—no matter what I do to my body from here on in—MRI. *Note: Yes, this is one of those first-person accounts, and usually I hate first-person accounts by columnists. Unless it's titled "My Wild Weekend of Hot Monkey Love with Heidi Klum," you could probably care less. But THIS... you need to know. If you are...

- Claustrophobic

- A wuss

- Both (see: Me)

Do not do this! Just have the darn surgery. Or be content with the use of one arm.

I had to get MRI'd as a result of a tragic tubing accident at my cottage last summer. (Hey, did you know that if you flip a tube at 30 miles an hour and don't let go... eventually it will flip back up? Of course, your arms will now be longer than Sasquatch's, and you'll never be able to lift a fork again, but it's still pretty cool.) Anyway, I shredded some shoulder ligament, or cartilage, or muscle, or something. And after X-rays revealed nothing, the orthopedic sadist, sorry, surgeon recommended the MRI.

This was not a concern. I'd had surgery before. I've dislocated shoulders and torn knees. Not to mention my pectoral implants. I could surely handle some puny medical test.

Or not.

I'll skip the boring science part (mainly because I don't understand it). All you really need to know is that an MRI is a giant magnetic cylinder, a couple of metres high, a couple of metres wide, and maybe three metres long, with a round hole in the middle where your body fits in. So, basically a giant coffin. Somehow, it's able to take 3-D images of your tissue. (NOTE: Lower body MRI's are no problem, as you get to keep your head out of the machine. It's the upper-body injuries where you get the pleasurable buried-alive experience.)

I'd heard the wait was several months' long. I wish. It only took six weeks before I was outside the death chamber at a Toronto hospital, being prepped by some guy named Ken, the MRI Grim Reaper.

"Ever work with metal... welding, etc?" Ken asks. Yes, I was a welder, Ken, but my real passion was dancing. *"He's a maniac! Maniac... On the floor...and he's dancing like he's never danced before..."* Sorry. *Flashdance* moment.

"No, Ken, I've never been a welder... But why does it matter?"

"Because if small particles of metal are in your body, they may be affected by the magnets and..."

And what, Ken? Suck my body into the vortex of the machine, killing me instantly? What if I swallowed a freakin' nickel when I was two, Ken? When you're scraping my innards off the cylinder after the magnets suck it out of my body, are you going to say, "Poor guy, should have told us about the nickel!?!"

Eventually, Ken convinced me my metal content should be low enough to avoid horrible disfiguration. So I lay down, he contorted my arm to his sadistic satisfaction, told me not to move a millimetre. For the next 35 minutes.

"Sorry, we're running late today," Ken small-talked as he got ready to send me in. "We had some problems earlier."

Problems? What the hell does that mean, Ken? Problems... like the machine leaked some magnetic radiation and turned the last patient to slime? What problems, Ken?!?

"We had a patient... umm... have some trouble... and... uhh... it took a while."

OK Ken, now you're freaking me out. Define "trouble," Ken.

"It just can be a little uncomfortable for some people, and if you stop the test at any time, you have to start all over again. Which we had to do five or six times with the patient this morning."

Fine. It was probably some old neurotic fraidy-cat. I'm a healthy, brave He-man. There will not be trouble.

And there wasn't. At least not for the first three or four seconds.

Here's a transcription of my thoughts as Ken sent me into the cylinder:

"OK, here we go. No problem... Just keep the eyes shut and relax. Hey, this is kind of cool. I feel like Sigourney Weaver in that sleep chamber in *Aliens*. Let's open the eyes. HOLY CRAP! My nose is almost touching the top. This is a freakin' tomb! I can't breathe! OUT! OUT NOW! MOMMY!!!"

They give you a panic button to hit. I was ready to squeeze it roughly nine seconds in, which might have been a record. I could have been the Usain Bolt of MRI. But then Ken's voice came through the speaker.

"Just relax and breathe," he said. Apparently Ken could sense I was about to have a seizure.

"We're going to start now. There's going to be about seven or eight of these... lasting anywhere from two to four minutes. You're going to hear some very loud noises throughout the tests. Don't be concerned."

Oh, I'm way past concerned, Ken. I'm not sure how to describe the noises. There were actually several. First, this low moaning, like whales mating (not that I know what whales sound like when they mate... they might scream BOO-YAH! for all I know). Then an annoying tapping, like Morse code. Tap tap tap... U... tap tap tap tap R... tap tap tap tap tap tap tap tap tap DEAD! That's it! U-R Dead! Oh crap.

And finally, the chorus: An opus of the loudest and most annoying buzzing noises in the history of sound. Like a million alarm clocks. And no snooze button to be found. It was painful. Worse than anything I'd ever heard. Even John Tesh's Greatest Hits. And so it went for a full half-hour. Whale moans. Tap-tap-tap. BUZZ-BUZZ. All as loud as if my head was up against the speaker at a Nine Inch Nails concert. Though I suppose the migraine it gave me helped me temporarily forget that I couldn't breathe and was about to die.

Somehow I didn't. I survived. Which, at that moment anyway, felt like the single greatest accomplishment of my adult life.

"How was it?" Ken asked, as he pulled me out of his Chamber of Horrors.

Fan-freakin'-tastic, Ken. You sicko.

To sum up, MRIs suck. Put it this way. If America really wanted those Al Qaeda prisoners at Guantanamo to talk... they should have given them an MRI.

"All right, NOW tell us where Bin Laden is... Oh and, by the way, you have a slight tear of your left posterior deltoid."

I haven't got the results back yet. With my luck, it will be "INCONCLUSIVE. FURTHER TESTS NEEDED."

Fat chance. I'd rather amputate.

• • •

Postscript: I was diagnosed with a small tear in my labrum, not bad enough to require surgery. We fixed it with a few months of physiotherapy. I was also self-diagnosed with claustrophobia, for which I blame Ken. He haunts my dreams to this day.

PATRICK ROY'S RIDE

October 2006

I feel like I'm on an episode of *Pimp My Bus.*

We are cruising through eastern Quebec with the Memorial Cup Champion Quebec Remparts, who are, by junior hockey standards, livin' large-antic.

They have satellite TV (at this moment tuned to the *SportsCenter* morning loop with the volume down and the tunes playing, and for the record, Dan O'Toole is hilarious on mute), a DVD player and those big spacious cushy seats with enough room between rows that Yao Ming could stretch out.

"I wanted to make this like a pro-team environment," says the second winningest goalie in NHL history, his feet resting on a closed cooler, the contents of which I will never discover before I jump off the bus halfway to Val d'Or. (Could be food. Could be beer. Could be the body of a hitchhiker. I mean... he'd never get caught. Even if they get pulled over, what cop is going to ask Patrick Roy to take his feet off the cooler? These are the things you ponder on long bus trips.)

This is Roy's new life.

A guy who I always imagined would be lounging by a pool at a mansion in Florida, playing 36 holes a day on some posh private billionaire's track, is, instead, taking 13-hour bus rides across eastern Canada, coaching a bunch of teenagers.

"I'm a lot simpler than people think," he says, staring out the window. (OK, I can't remember if he was actually staring out the window when he said that, but quotes always sound much deeper when the guy is staring out the window.)

"I enjoyed staying at The Ritz-Carlton and eating filet mignon every night, but there's nothing wrong with spaghetti and motels."

Yes, Patrick Roy digs the Pizza Hut in Chicoutimi, and the Super 8 in Shawinigan. Who knew? And as we ride and talk, he seems more content than any former hockey star I've ever met.

"I could not think of a better way to spend my retirement," he says.

But hold on. This cannot be the end game. He is not Brian Kilrea. Roy has always wanted more. So we cut to the chase.

"Do you want to be the head coach or GM of the Montreal Canadiens?"

I would ask this question three different times in the span of two minutes, never quite certain I got an answer. First try:

"I'm very happy in Quebec."

"That doesn't really answer my..."

"I think they have a very good coach, he's a friend of mine and I think they have the best person as a GM in Montreal. I think they will be there for a very long time."

"But what if they weren't?"

"If and if, eh? I guess my aunt would be my uncle. You could ask me the same question five years from now and maybe I'll have a different answer."

Oh, I believe he would. Let's be clear. This is nothing but a hunch. I know Roy about as well as I know... say... Evangeline Lilly. Which is (sadly), not at all (despite numerous dreams to the contrary, most of which involve me running towards her yelling, "Open the hatch! Open the hatch!").

But I bet you Patrick wants it.

In fact, I bet he wants it bad. I bet the way he left Montreal is the one single biggest regret in his hockey life, no matter how well it turned out in Colorado. I bet going back to the Canadiens would right that wrong in his mind.

I bet it's inevitable.

"I had a talk with Carbo," Roy says. "He asked me if I want to join him. It was not an official offer, but I explained to him, I like what I'm doing. I touch everything here. I'm involved in every department of this club and I like that." So, not yet. And he's right. Gainey and Carbonneau are talented hockey people who could be around for a while.

But someday, I bet, the Canadiens will come calling. And they'll give Roy the control he wants. And he will leap at it. And when that day comes?

I wouldn't bet against him.

• • •

Postscript: As the time of publication, Roy is still riding the buses. Guy Carbonneau was fired by the Canadiens at the end of the 2009 season, and replaced by Jacques Martin. Bob Gainey is no longer GM of the Habs. Roy was reportedly offered the dual job of coach/ general manager with the Colorado Avalanche, but turned it down. One tidbit I found out two years too late for this column: A hotel employee in PEI told me that Roy left his favourite pillow at their hotel during a road trip with his team. He realized it only after the bus was two hours away. He turned the bus around, and returned to get the pillow.

THE BOYS OF SUMMER

August 2002

So, we're sitting in silence at the edge of the dock, our dangling feet making the only ripples on an otherwise glass tabletop lake, and the morning is darn near perfect, and suddenly he says: "Dad, what's summer?"

Hmmm. OK.

Buddy, summer is that smile you gave me when you finally hit the giant plastic yellow ball with the giant plastic red bat.

Summer is fantasizing that your team will sign all the big name free agents.

And then watching them getting outbid for Kip Miller.

Summer is watching your 11-year-old nephew get up on water skis after two years of failure, and several more of abstinence through fear, then seeing him throw his arms in the air, whoopin' and hollerin' and struttin' off the dock like he just beat Roy Jones Jr.

Summer is your first-ever 39 on the front. Followed by your 132nd-ever 54 on the back.

Summer is seeing the same nephew string and bait his own rod, cast like he was Redford in *A River Runs Through It*, and then, after landing a three-inch sunfish, scream for his dad to take it off the hook for him.

Summer is about Bud (weiser). Summer is not about Bud (Selig). Or Donald Fehr. Summer is not about either one of them.

Summer is taking your girl to one of the last drive-ins left in the Western world, getting giddy when you find out it's showing *Minority Report*, then screaming like Love-Hewitt when you realize the first half of the double-bill is *Secrets of the Ya-Ya Sisterhood*.

Summer is... about six months too short.

Summer is listening to your favourite jock-talk radio host do an hour on the Tour de France because it's the day after the All-Star Game, the ultimate sports dead zone, and he's got nothing else. Nada. *"The lines are open if you'd like to call in. Please call in. Please."*

Summer is letting your baby daughter try her first Mr. Freezie, and give you a look like: "Dang! You've been holding out on me. Any chance we can stock up Mom's left nipple with this stuff?"

Summer is doing a Pete Rose on Ray Fosse's bowl-over-the-catcher-smack to score the winning run... in the coed softball game at the company picnic, and the catcher is Helen, a 47-year-old mother of three in a sundress. Helen, your boss's secretary.

Summer is looking for a new job.

Summer is watching the boy-next-door splash and frolic all afternoon in his tiny plastic Barney pool. The boy is 36. His kids are away at camp.

Summer is doing your best Tiger fist-pump after reaching the green in two.

... On a par three.

Summer is going camping for the weekend to get away from it all. Then spending most of Saturday on your cell phone with your Roto-League buddies desperately trying to deal Roger Cedeno.

Summer is tasting a jumbo ballpark frank, blanketed in onions and sauerkraut and every condiment known to man. And then tasting it over and over again over the next three to five days.

Summer is 9:13 p.m. And still enough light to hit one more bucket of balls.

Summer is the blonde in the tank top on the roller blades who is about to cause a 32-car pile-up. She should be on Maaco's payroll. She is carnage waiting to happen.

Summer is the first two weeks of training camp, when even the Bengals can dream.

Summer is this very moment, with you and me and the sun and the lake, and the wish that autumn and everything after didn't exist. Or at least could hold off a while.

"Dad," he says after a long silence. "What's autumn?"

• • •

Postscript: Readers often ask me if I make these scenes up. I don't. My three-year-old really did ask, "Dad, what's summer?" on the dock that morning. But my answer certainly wasn't as profound as the column. I had to read it to him two days later, after I wrote it. I was expecting some big "now I understand" hug at the end. But if I remember correctly, I think he said something like, "Daddy, you write dumb stuff." Most would say that's a fair assessment.

PRE-GAME PERIL

October 2007

Forget for a moment the headshots, the hits from behind, the separated shoulders from fighting. The latest grave danger in hockey is... well... it isn't even... from playing hockey.

It's from playing soccer before playing hockey.

Carolina Hurricanes forward Erik Cole was trying to juggle a soccer ball before a game Saturday night in Philadelphia. His foot met concrete instead of ball. Owweee (or some expletive-laden synonym).

Cole reportedly yelled in agony and had to be carried away by teammates. And unlike most soccer players who go down, he wasn't faking. There was no fracture, but he's out of the lineup at least a week.

Cole was taking part in a popular pre-game hockey ritual called "two-touch," where a group of teammates stand in a circle trying to keep a soccer ball in the air. You can touch the ball twice, but then must pass to a teammate. (Note: "Two-touch" has different meanings in different cities. For example, in Toronto, it refers to the number of times the Leafs touch the puck in their own end each game.)

Last season, Flyers (then Predators) forward Scott Hartnell did almost exactly the same thing as Cole. He missed six weeks with a broken foot. And before a first round playoff game last spring, Sabres forward Maxim Afinogenov banged his head on the concrete playing circle-footie, giving sad new meaning to the term cement-head. Afinogenov played that night, but was scratched in the next round against the Rangers.

"I don't think he was right for a little while after that," Lindy Ruff admitted months later.

Concrete can do that to a brain.

This is becoming an epidemic, people! Soccer hasn't seen players go down this often since Ronaldo. Or Rivaldo. Or Geraldo... Rivera. (I have no idea what that means, but it rhymed. And that was enough for me.) This must stop, boys! You are hockey players. That's dangerous enough. You don't need to be leaping for headers when there's an overhanging metal pipe. Ride the bike to warm up. Do yoga. Make out with a groupie. Anything!

When they say "Bend it like Beckham", they mean the ball, not your fibula.

Some NHL coaches are considering banning the game. I would simply manage the soccer-circle roster carefully.

"Laraque, you can play with the soccer ball. Crosby, no."

Of course, the problem isn't really the game. It's where the game is played: in small tunnels outside dressing rooms where there is mostly just cement and steel and... stuff that really hurts when you run into it. What NHL arenas really need is a two-touch court with padded walls and Nerf balls. Or put up one of those bouncy castles my kids jump on at the fair.

"Ovechkin, you have to get dressed! The team is on the ice!"

"Wheeeeeeeeeeeeee!"

Until something is done about this pre-game footie fetish, the carnage will continue. And hockey fans will have one more reason to hate soccer.

• • •

Postscript: *December 28, 2008—Toronto Maple Leafs forward Matt Stajan sent to hospital with eye injury after being hit with ball in soccer warm-up. March 12, 2009—New York Islander Kurtis McLean ruptures Achilles tendon during pre-game soccer warm-up. November 1, 2009—Vancouver Canuck Michael Grabner severely injures ankle playing pre-game soccer. Kids, I can't help you if you refuse to listen.*

THE BRADY INTERVIEW

February 2002

He was less than a first down away, and heading my way. Helmet off, hair champagne-drenched, eyes glazed in delirium.

The empty stool next to me was beckoning. At least I was beckoning it to beckon him. If I could just pry his attention away from the two dozen other reporters, and handlers, and hangers-on, hounding and surrounding him as he strolled towards the tunnel, I might have a shot at a one-on-one interview.

"Hey, Tom!" I bellowed. "Got a minute? We're live across Canada!"

Tom Brady turned and started towards me, smiling the smile of a 24-year-old who had just been given the keys to a shiny new...

World.

• • •

Sorry, Kelly Clarkson, but the real American Idol was crowned that Super Bowl Sunday seven months ago.

Sure, some thought he would be football's Chumbawamba. One huge hit and gone. But watching him dissect the Steelers Monday night, Tom Brady looked like he just might have a longer run than Marsha and his other namesakes did in syndication. And all I kept thinking about was that night in Naw'lins.

It had been barely a half-hour since Boston Tom became Broadway Joe, leading the Patriots to an upset of Namathian proportions. We were doing live post-game coverage on the carpet of the Superdome, right about the spot where Vinatieri's walk-off field goal had landed.

A few straggling confetti flakes were still falling from the rafters as Brady came towards us. Instantly... all those lame-brained post-game questions swirled around my head.

"How does it feel, Tom?"

Owwwch. The weakest of openers. Heck, Ahmad Rashad probes deeper than that. But geez, wouldn't you like to know? How could it possibly feel? Leading your team down the field in the final buck and change of the biggest game in the galaxy... to complete the most improbable, unfathomable season of any quarterback in history... to win the dang Super Bowl... and the Super Bowl MVP... and the car that goes with it... and the mega-money extension that would follow... Oh yeah, and the phone number of any *Maxim* covergirl you want.

How did it feel? Pretty freakin' fantastic, would be my educated guess.

"How'd you do it, Tom?"

We'd all memorized this part long ago. He was a draft afterthought, a sixth rounder who, if he made the roster at all, would likely stand on the sidelines in an embarrassingly clean uniform, wearing a ball cap for the next five years. But he worked his way up from 4th string, and then suddenly, 1st string was in the hospital with a collapsed lung.

Opportunity knocked, and Tommy Boy busted down the door. Brady never bothered to try to figure out how to do it. Too complicated. He just did it.

"Weren't you nervous, Tom?"

About as much as Tiger in a two-dollar Nassau. In those final few pre-game minutes in the locker room, somewhere between Paul McCartney and Mariah Carey, while some players vomited, and others head-butted, Brady napped.

"What's next, Tom?"

Well, let's see. An all-night party, followed by an 8:30 a.m. MVP news conference, followed by a jet to *Disney World*, followed by a parade with Mickey, followed by a flight to Boston, followed by a parade with the Patriots, followed by a flight to Hawaii, followed by a Pro Bowl practice.

And that was just the first 48 hours. Over the next few months, Brady would:

- Turn down Tara Reid (who needs a slice of American Pie, when you can have the whole thing?).

- Pose for the cover of *SI* shirtless (and take a ribbing about it for the next four months and counting).

- Get on the Donald Trump jet and fly to Miss USA 2002 where apparently every contestant's mother would beg him to date her daughter.

- Hang with Hef and the girls at the Playboy Mansion.

- Break up with his girlfriend (no official confirmation of the connection between this and the preceding two events, but you figure it out).

- Sign a bunch of endorsement deals (including Dunkin' Donuts, which should really get the O-line jealous).

- Spawn about a million Brady-worshipping websites featuring proclamations like the following from "absolutebrady.com"

"… I finally believe again, the whole fairytale story and it has a lot to do with a man named Brady… Tom is the modern version of the knight in shining armor, the prince charming of the 21st century. He brought back what was once thought to be extinct."

Ah, Tom. I think she might like you.

So, basically, his summer was one long Nelly video. And this from a guy who couldn't get into a fitness club last year because they didn't believe he was really an NFL player.

"Will this change you, Tom?"

"Oh yeah, he's changed all right," says Patriots fullback Marc Edwards, the morning after the champs' opening night destruction of the Steelers.

"His wallet's a lot thicker. Oh, and he's a little more confident, not that it was a problem before. But besides that, he's exactly the same guy."

• • •

I try to answer these questions now, seven months later, because I never got to ask them that Super Sunday in Lousiana.

As Brady turned to come towards me, the giant mosh pit of PR people and press and posse swept him up and carried him right on by. The new American Idol glanced back over his shoulder and gave me a smile and a "Sorry, it's out of my hands" shrug as the horde whisked him into the tunnel, and on to a new life that neither he, nor we, could possibly imagine.

• • •

Postscript: Whatever he did imagine back then, reality probably surpassed it. In the eight years since this column was written, Brady has added two more Super Bowl rings, married supermodel Gisele Bundchen, made more than $100 million in salary and endorsements, and become one of the greatest quarterbacks in football history.

THE REAL
HOCKEYTOWN

December 2003

Peter and Markus meet me at the airport.

How cool is that? Two steps off the plane and there they are! The two best players in the world last year, waving and smiling like I was their homey. (How do you say homey in Swedish? These things keep me up at night.) Makes a guy feel special to get that kind of greeting.

By the way, they are cardboard.

The real Forsberg and Naslund left their hometown weeks ago. Back to North America to start chasing Stanleys and Harts. So their life-size cardboard cut-outs are left to greet every visitor (and trust me, there aren't many) who lands at the tiny strip of concrete passed off as an airport. (You know an airport is small when the pilot, the baggage handler, and the rent-a-car dude, are the same guy.)

Welcome to Ornskoldsvik, Sweden, where they make pulp and paper, and hockey players. If Detroit is Hockeytown USA, then O-vik (please don't make me type the whole thing again) is Hockeytown, EARTH. No place on the planet produces more NHLers per capita than this little port on the Baltic Sea, 500 kilometres north of Stockholm.

Ladies and gentlemen, introducing your O-vik starting lineup: Forsberg, Naslund, Henrik Sedin, Daniel Sedin, Niklas Sundstrom, Sammy Pahlsson, Mattias Timander, Hans Jonsson, Anders Ericksson, Andreas Salomonsson, Per Svartvadet.

OK, so they aren't all Hart Trophy candidates, but that's 11 guys who played in The Show last year from a town smaller than Moose Jaw.

In O-vik, either you are, you are related to, your Dad coached, your sister dated, or the guy who gave you a wedgie back in Grade 6 is, an NHL player. I tried to play Six Degrees of Marcus Naslund with the locals, and never got beyond one.

"Marcus? I used to cut his hair!"

"I delivered his paper!"

"I had his love-child!"

(Coming from a drunken elderly man at the local pub, I suspect the latter may not have been accurate.)

This whole town has a Hockey Mojo. Or make that Modo. That's O-vik's professional club, the one that graduated Naslund, Forsberg, the Sedins and the rest to the NHL.

But it's more than the team. It's the system. Kids can join Modo at six. They get top-level training all the way up, and the best of them will get to attend... get this... Hockey High School.

Hockey High School??? Do detentions last two or five minutes depending on the severity of the offense?

I tag along with Oscar Hedman, one of the best 17-year-old defencemen in Sweden as he heads to class: math, then computers, then... well... hockey. First to the rink for 90 minutes of practice, then another half-hour in the weight room, all during school hours. He'll be graded just like every other class.

"Hey, Oscar, how'd you do on your penalty-killing mid-term?"

O-vik's HHS is one of only two in Sweden, and another reason the town is an NHL breeding ground.

But it's more than that. Heck, it has to be! Two Hart finalists?!? Six first-rounders?!? In O-vik, babies aren't just born with a stick in their hands, they cut the cord with a wicked backhand. The first phone number a teenage boy gets is an agent's. Even the grandmas have mullets. Must be the water.

"No, the food!" shouts Danno Sternad, as he shows me around his Italian restaurant, Momma Mia's (which I believe is one of only 18 million Italian restaurants in the world named Momma Mia's. Whoever Momma Mia is, I hope she gets a cut).

Danno's place doubles as a shrine to O-vik hockey. His walls are lined with autographed jerseys from all the hometown heroes, most of whom still drop by every couple of weeks in the off-season.

"I even make a special dish for them, Hockey Pasta!" he yells gleefully.

For the record, it's gnocchi mixed with veggies, ox meat and Gorgonzola cheese. And it works! I wolfed down a plate, and on the way home, deked out a lady with a baby carriage and hip-checked a guy with a cane.

Yes in O-vik, you are literally fed hockey. And they eat it up.

And just wait 'til next year! If the NHL shuts down, they are all talking about playing for Modo. Forsberg, Naslund, the Sedins. All of them.

So lockout or not, there will be NHL hockey to watch next year. It'll just be a helluva commute.

• • •

Postscript: That teenager I followed around in O-vik, Oscar Hedman, has turned into a very good professional player in Sweden. When I was there, he kept saying, "You should see my little brother play." That little brother turned out to be Victor Hedman, the second overall pick in the 2009 NHL Draft, and likely a future Norris Trophy winner for the Tampa Bay Lightning.

NO SHAME IN A
STRANGE NAME

March 2000

Sports fans beware. A dangerous precedent has been set which could
severely hamper our enjoyment of the games we love. The disturbing
news comes out of Tegucigalpa, Honduras, where the National Elec-
toral Tribunal is attempting to... brace yourself... ban wacky names!

Who in the Stubby Clapp do they think they are?!? Who died and
made them God Shammgod?!?

Apparently, the Hondurans are worried about an outbreak of
"extravagant or offensive" names being registered of late. They cite
examples like Bujia (Spark Plug) and Llanta de Milagro (Miracle Tire).

"Look at the little fella, honey! He looks just like the front-left
rubber on my '73 Pinto! I shall call him Miracle Tire."

Sure his parents have issues, but the Honduran government need
not worry about little Miracle Tire. He'll be fine, probably score a six-
figure Goodyear endorsement deal by the time he's three.

Kids with funny names might get teased a little on the playground, might take a couple of extra shots to the head in dodgeball,

but when they grow up and play college or pro, they make us giggle like Tickle Me Elmo.

Good names create good characters at a time when good characters (and good character for that matter) are hard to come by.

Would this really be a free world without World B. Free? An original name can put an ordinary athlete on the (Scientific) Mapp (basketball). Even if a name sounds Ickey (Woods, football), it's still Cool (Papa Bell, baseball) and (Xree) Hipp (basketball).

There are names for the Beavis and Butthead crowd: Dick Trickle (auto racing), Woodie Held (baseball), Harry Colon (football).

"Heh, heh. You said colon. Heh, heh."

There are names that just belong together: "Fair Hooker (football), meet Bimbo Coles (baseball)."

There are names where you better be good: Fabulous Flournoy (basketball), Peerless Price (football), Majestic Mapp (brother of Scientific, also basketball). Wonderful Monds (football) and son Wonderful Terrific Monds (baseball). And there are names where you're good in spite of yourself: Gene Krapp (baseball), Pooh Richardson (basketball), Eddie Stanky (baseball).

The best names are the ones that just roll off the (Reggie) Tongue (football). Repeat after me: Ford Frick (baseball). Hakan Loob (hockey). Minnie Minoso (baseball). Baskerville Holmes (basketball). Kwaku Boateng (high jumper). Pardee Abadee (basketball). Carlester Crumpler (football). Guppy Troup (bowling).

It's fun for the whole family! You could make an all-name board game. Let's call Milton Bradley (baseball)!

Of course, originality isn't for everyone. Just ask George Foreman's sons: George, George, George, George and George. Must be confusing opening gifts on Christmas morning. Then again, he probably gives them all a grill anyway.

George is no less egomaniacal than Roger Clemens, who gave his four boys names starting with "K" (Kory, Koby, Kacy and Kody) in honor of all his strikeouts. After his two losses in the AL Division Series, perhaps Larry, Lenny, Leo and Ludwig would have been more appropriate.

I always wanted to name my first child after an athlete. So as we played the name-game last year awaiting the birth of our son, and my wife was pondering the Zacharys and Joshuas, I was after something with attitude. Maybe Latrell.

"Honey, the baby's choking the dog again!"

She wouldn't go for it.

"What about Mookie?" I pleaded. "No Mookie ever choked anybody. Everybody loves a Mookie!"

Didn't fly.

"Mookie is a name for a Muppet," she said, "not a man."

Sure, tell that to Mrs. Blaylock and Mrs. Wilson.

We did eventually settle on something, but it's not important. What is important is for all sports fans to stand up and quash this Honduran proposal before it spreads. It's a (Gus) Krock (baseball). They seem to have their (Ed) Head (baseball) stuck between their (Maurice) Cheeks (basketball).

Oops. Sorry. Gotta go. My baby is crying again. Cute little fella never shuts up.

"Coming, Keyshawn!"

• • •

Postscript: If I had to update this column, I'd probably change the last line to "Coming, Terrell!" By the way, the Hondurans were apparently ahead of their time in calling for a lame-name ban. In 2009, the Dominican Republic followed suit, after parents started naming their kids things like "Rambo Weed," "Dear Pineapple," and "Iloveyou Lover." Whatever happened to "Steve"?

THE JETER METER

October 2001

No offense to John Malkovich, who is right up there with Christopher Walken and the guy who played Buffalo Bill in *Silence of the Lambs* on my all-time favourite psycho list, but if you were to find a porthole into someone's brain, would there be anything better right now than "Being Derek Jeter"?

Methinks not. (Being Heidi Klum would be interesting, too, but in an entirely different context.)

It's male nature to fantasize about being someone else. We've all wished we were the superstar shortstop, or part of a dynasty, or rich beyond comprehension or dating Miss Universe. But heck, none of us are bold enough to dream of having *all of that.*

Jeter does.

He's got great glove, great bat, more rings than Liberace, a Monopoly-money contract (I believe he actually does own Park Place), a Rolodex full of supermodels and not a single felony arrest.

The King of New York. At 27.

Dang, I'm jealous.

For purely scientific purposes, let's compare Jeter's ridiculously charmed life to that of an average male Shmoe. Any volunteers? Fine. I'll be your lab monkey.

DEREK JETER

DJ: Gets 200 pieces of fan mail a day.

DJ: Dated Mariah Carey, walked out after four months.

DJ: Currently seeing Miss Universe Lara Dutta.

DJ: Has four World Series rings

DJ: Presented with key to New York City by Mayor Giuliani.

DJ: Has 10-year, $189-million contract.

DJ: Makes cover of *GQ* in Gucci suit.

DJ: Often called "five-tool player."

JAMES DUTHIE

JD: Gets 200 pieces of junk mail a day.

JD: Took date to Mariah Carey movie *Glitter*, walked out after 20 minutes.

JD: Once turned down by Miss Bud Light Daytona Beach.

JD: Still has Superfriends decoder ring from old Froot Loops box. Also considered getting eyebrow ring to try to look more "dangerous." That's about it.

JD: Presented with key to neighbour's apartment to clean cat litter while she was away.

JD: Needs one more stamp on card to get free sub at Subway.

JD: Still waiting for Le Chateau to bring back Parachute pants.

JD: Often called "tool."

DJ: Made one of the great defensive plays of all time to help win 2001 American League Championship Series.

JD: Bowled over chubby female catcher to score meaning-less run in 1997 Coed Slo-pitch Softball Consolation Final. Made her cry.

Wow, I actually match up pretty well. But it's still clear why Jeter has earned his place as the new standard for male envy. Thus, we proudly introduce the **Jeter Meter**.

It's a simple scale, designed to help males rate the celebrities, sports or otherwise, who they dream of being. Since Jeter himself is the optimum target on the **Jeter Meter**, he would rate a 10. Other celebrities whose lives you envy get rated accordingly.

For example, on my **Jeter Meter**, Kobe Bryant is a solid 8. J-Lo's husband has come from nowhere to grab a 9. P. Diddy, on the other hand, has dropped to a 5. Felony gun charges have that effect. Dustin Diamond is a 2 (he would have been a 1, but in *Saved by the Bell: The New Class*, his vivid portrayal of Screech's slow descent into Hell was riveting).

Before you create your own Jeter Meter, there's one other detail I neglected to mention. Obviously, it's difficult to make subjective rankings without a starting point. If Derek Jeter is the maximum (10) on our fantasy trading-places scale, there has to be a celebrity minimum (1).

I'm going with Carrot Top.

• • •

Postscript: When I wrote this column, Jeter had won three World Series titles in his first five big league seasons, and was four wins away from his fourth. The Yankees lost that year to Arizona, and didn't win another title until 2009. Jeter remains a ridiculously talented, classy, rich superstar. Last I heard of Carrot Top, he was headlining at the Luxor in Vegas, and had more plastic surgery than Joan Rivers, Burt Reynolds, and Pamela Anderson combined. The Jeter Meter is still very much intact.

REMEMBERING WHEELS

February 2007

If you could watch one hockey player, past or present, play a game, who would it be? Gretzky at 21? Orr, with knees scar-free? The Rocket, at his angry, eyes-blazing best? Crosby, right now? I'm often asked that question. And I was never sure of the answer. Until now. It is none of the above.

If I could watch one player lace up the skates and play a game, I would choose a skinny left-winger from Guelph, Ontario.

A player who moved so fast, they called him Wheels.

A terrific hockey mind who, by the age of 10, had already patented his own move: carrying the puck swiftly into the opposing zone, then spinning around and sending it back to his point man, leading to countless chances for his team.

A leader, so popular in the room, a former coach says when he walked in for practice, there would be a chorus of "Sit here! Sit next to me!"

A coach's dream, always shining his shoes to make sure he looked proper when he arrived at the rink. And so obsessed with being on time, he wore a digital watch with a face big enough to dwarf his little arms.

An offensive dynamo who scored 12 goals in one seven-game span this season, amazing considering he always preferred being a playmaker.

A natural athlete who was also a whiz at soccer, football, track and pretty much everything he tried.

An always-smiling charmer who, even when he tried to boast, couldn't help but turn it into a joke.

"I'm the best athlete in my school," he once said. "Then again, my school is really small."

A kid who lived and breathed hockey from the second he woke 'til the moment he hit the pillow, exhausted after playing hours a day.

But here's the rub. This hockey player I'd love to see play again... I never saw him play.

Everything I know about him comes from the stories I've been told over the past week by teammates, coaches, friends and family.

His name was Nicholas Lambden. Two Sundays ago, he was doing something every one of us who has played outdoor pick-up hockey has done hundreds of times: digging for a puck in the snow. A shot from a nearby game struck him in the head. It was a freak, million-to-one accident.

And it killed him.

Nick was 10 years old—*10 years old*.

Last Friday, the Guelph Atom AA Junior Storm should have been excitedly preparing for the next round of their playoffs. Instead, they were walking up the aisle of a church, past the coffin with their team-mate's No. 12 sweater draped over it, laying their sticks next to Nick's. Later, they'd talk about how happy he'd been after scoring the tying goal late in what would be a thrilling OT win that past Saturday. His last game.

Nick loved hockey. Loved the Leafs. Worshipped Mats Sundin, Sidney Crosby and Alexander Ovechkin. He dreamed of being just like them, of someday being talked about on TSN. Consider it done, Wheels.

I thank all of his friends for sharing their memories this week. But each new gut-wrenching phone call, each heart-breaking e-mail that pops up in the inbox makes me wish I could have met Nick, and watched him play the game he loved so much.

And makes me curse the fact I never will.

• • •

Postscript: The story about Nick's death was a tiny blurb in my Monday morning paper. Our country is huge, but we like to think our hockey community is small and tight. So I 411ed the family's name and called, feeling Nick deserved more than a one-paragraph wire story. This column provoked an outpouring of sympathy and grief from hockey fans across the country. The following column ran exactly two years later.

REMEMBERING WHEELS, PART 2

February 2009

The late afternoon was sunny, and crisp, and begging for shinny.

This is our first winter in a new town, and my nine-year-old boy had been asking me for weeks to find him an outdoor rink. I hadn't, and for that, like Denis Lemieux, I feel shame. Between the boy's rep hockey, his two sisters' dance classes, swimming lessons, Mom's yoga and Dad spending all his nights asking other men in makeup if Lecavalier should be traded, there never seems to be time to find a patch of ice. And just... play.

But last Monday after school, all the Daytimers were magically clear. So when the kid next door came calling, stick and skates in hand, saying there was a dandy, full-size rink at a school just a few blocks away, we were in toques and longjohns at Usain Bolt-speed.

My boy asked if he should bring his helmet, and I gave him that annoying, fatherly, "What do you think?" stare. He didn't argue.

Until we got to the rink.

I was dumbfounded. There must have been 20 kids on the ice, playing two separate games. The youngest was probably eight or nine, the oldest well into his teens. And not a single one was wearing a helmet.

"See, Dad, why can't I just wear my hat?"

I'm not sure I even answered. All I could think about was Wheels.

Nicholas "Wheels" Lambden was a 10-year-old dynamo of a hockey player from Guelph, Ontario. He had blond hair and a wide grin that belonged in a milk commercial. The nickname, of course, came from his speed. No matter what the sport, the boy could fly.

Two winters ago, Nick was playing shinny on a rink in a park near his house. He was digging a puck out of a snowbank when a shot from a nearby game struck him in the head, and killed him.

"You have a heartbeat, so you keep living, but I miss him every moment," says Andrew Lambden, Nick's father, as the family approaches the two-year anniversary of Nick's death. "I see him, hear him, touch him in my imagination. The sadness is completely overwhelming."

I had thought of Nick often over the past two years. I still have the black armband one of his teammates handed me after I came to watch them play a few weeks later. And I remember the unspeakable heartbreak in his Mom Susan's voice when I spoke with her the night after his passing. Between the tears, she asked me for one thing: to tell all parents to make sure their kids wear helmets whenever they play hockey.

That wish became part of the Lambden's focus in keeping Nick's memory alive. They created a foundation in his honor, and have pushed for laws to make helmets mandatory on outdoor rinks. Nick's foundation donated 18-inch-high nets, to help keep shots low, and the City of Guelph legislated that they be the only kind used on the ice in their parks. But mandatory helmets have been a trickier issue in this country.

"It's unbelievable that many kids still aren't wearing them," says Andrew Lambden. "My greatest fear is that it will happen to someone else. To think that it is preventable and yet we're doing very little about it is troubling. No one would ever allow their kids to play without a helmet indoors, and yet outdoors we seem to say 'It's Canada, it's our national pastime, there is ice everywhere, and we can't control it.'"

"I know why Nick didn't have his on that day," says Susan Lambden. "It was freezing out, just like today, and he wanted his hat on to keep his ears warm. With Nick's foundation, we've been working on finding liners that work under helmets to keep you warm. That would help. But no matter what, kids just have to put the helmets on. I just wish everyone could understand that... everything can change in a split second."

We all loved the feeling of skating without the burden of that cumbersome lid. Growing up, we played shinny every night in the backyard of my friend Sylvain's house in Blackburn Hamlet. I don't think we ever wore helmets. Then again, we never wore them riding bikes either.

Do we overprotect our kids today? Absolutely. But it beats the hell out of the alternative. Ask the Lambdens. Even a million-to-one chance is too big a risk.

I didn't say anything to the other kids at the rink that afternoon. Didn't want to be the preachy stranger. I just sat my boy down on the snowbank, and reminded him of Nick's story. "I'm almost as old as he was," was his only response.

He quietly slipped on the helmet, and asked me to do up the snaps. Then he skated off into the fading afternoon light, with puck and stick, and infinite possibilities.

• • •

Postscript: I still receive e-mails from some of Nick's teammates and their parents, saying how much he is missed. Nick's foundation continues to work with various organizations, with the goal of providing opportunities for kids to play sports, in a safe environment. The foundation is currently fundraising to help build a new outdoor rink in front of the new city hall in Guelph.

HOCKEY'S FIRST
YOUTUBE LEGEND

May 2008

I believe I'm one of the few humans ever to have a documented meeting with Horn Chen, the Snuffleupagus of sports ownership. No one believed the reclusive former Ottawa Rough Riders proprietor existed until that day, when he made a brief cameo at a fan rally. I pinched him on live TV to prove he wasn't made of wax or computer-generated. It was exciting stuff. I felt like I'd captured a Bigfoot.

I thought of Chen this week while trying to chase down Fabian Brunnstrom, hockey's yeti... Loch Ness Monster... live alien... take your pick. For the better part of five months, the hockey world has been buzzing about this undrafted late-bloomer, who no one but a few scouts and Swedish puck bunnies have seen play.

The mysterious Brunnstrom never answered his cell phone when I tried to reach him this week, though I get so confused with Europe's continental area code, country code, city code... Morse code... thing. It's quite possible I was dialing a Thai massage parlor in Belgium. Again.

"I didn't just make him up," says Brunnstrom's agent, JP Barry, laughing. "He is real. He is a very skilled player with a lot of speed."

The only footage out there of Brunnstrom in action is grainy YouTube video, which has become his own Zapruder film. Here comes the wrist shot. Down and to the left. Down and to the left. It's impressive, though it took me three viewings to figure out which one was Brunnstrom.

The lack of video evidence on this 22-year-old Swedish Elite Leaguer has only added to the mystery and hype. Nowadays, we are used to knowing everything about our future hockey stars by the time they're shaving. John Tavares highlights started appearing on *SportsCenter* when he was 14. The World Juniors make most top prospects household names years before they don an NHL sweater. So the potential of an instant, out-of-nowhere, American Idol-ish star has fans in a frenzy. Brunnstrom is the most Googled Swede since Tiger's wife, and he's inspired endless chatter on NHL thread-sites.

"OMG did you see that move on the video! Nucks plz sign him!"—naslundfan.

"I'm praying for the Leafs to sign him. Sundin-Steen-Brunnstrom would be sick!"—snipecheeseallday.

"Give him 10 mill now and the Cup is ours, baby!"—hockeytown4ever.

So their expectation level for the kid is somewhere between Zetterberg and Jesus. Yes, folks, we have our first Internet-created hockey legend.

It's all Daniel Alfredsson's fault, really. The fact the Senators superstar also happened to be a late-bloomer from Sweden is enough for the bloghogs to proclaim Brunnstrom "The Next Alfie." That's what nine goals and 28 assists in 54 games in the Swedish Elite League gets you these days.

Fabian Fever hit new heights this week when he arrived in North America for a mini-tour of the teams he wants to play for. As many as 20 clubs have inquired about signing Brunnstrom, including Ottawa, though their interest has apparently waned. Vancouver almost had him signed until the Dave Nonis firing. Fabian's Fab Four shortlist now includes Dallas, Detroit, Montreal and Toronto (with Anaheim reportedly trying to make a late push).

You should have heard the chaos in our control room when they learned he was at the game in Dallas on Wednesday. Our cameras scoured the building, searching for the first (North American Exclusive!) Brunnstrom close-up. When they thought they'd found him, we had to do split-screen with his Internet photos, to make sure it was really him.

He was accompanied by a gorgeous blonde, which instantly made me wonder if the Stars were going that "extra mile" to sign him. Turns out it was his girlfriend, Sandy Rantzow, who happens to be a European women's karate champion. Let's hope it works out, because that could be a painful breakup.

The next night in Detroit, TSN's Ryan Rishaug landed the first Brunnstrom one-on-one (somewhere, Oprah is seething). When Ryan asked what type of game Brunnstrom will bring to the NHL, he replied: "I don't know if I'm ready for the NHL."

Oops. Clearly he wasn't behind the hype machine. He may want to enrol in the Sean Avery School of Self-Promotion.

"I think I'm an offensive-type player and I try to skate a lot," Brunnstrom added, likely realizing his first statement may have cost him a beach house and a Benz. He actually came across as a nice, nervous kid, somewhat overwhelmed by all the attention.

By all accounts, Brunnstrom is a good NHL prospect. Just how good is where the discussion gets gray. I suppose it's possible he could be the next Daniel Alfredsson. Or he may be the next Magnus Arvedson. Or he may be the most hyped AHLer in history. No one knows for sure.

It is rather odd that such a dynamic player is eating cheese nachos at NHL playoff games instead of playing for Sweden at the World Hockey Championship, though Swedish hockey politics might have something to do with that. (Word is they aren't fond of Fab-Mania. They prefer the more traditional pay-your-dues path to fame.)

For now, Brunnstrom remains a mystery wrapped in a riddle inside an enigma (apologies to Winston Churchill and Joe Pesci).

With his trip to Montreal completed, he'll likely decide sometime soon where he wants to play.

Parade details to follow shortly thereafter.

• • •

Postscript: Brunnstrom would eventually sign a two-year contract with the Dallas Stars, for almost $2.5 million a season. He scored a hat trick in his NHL debut on Oct. 14, 2009, but has been inconsistent since then. The Internet has since become a popular place for prospects to show off their skills, though it hasn't replaced actual scouting. Yet. "And with the 21st pick of the 2014 NHL Draft, Vancouver selects: that dude from Finland who did the cool backhand flip move on YouTube."

CAREER OPTIONS

November 2003

The Boy turned four today. So I figured it was about time to talk about the birds and the bees. Meaning the Eagles and the Bruins. (Plus all the other relevant sporting information a child should know.)

You see, he hit me with that, "Dad, when I grow up, I want to be a..." line.

But before he could finish, I thought I'd offer up a few helpful suggestions.

He is only four after all. A child needs guidance.

"You could grow up to be a hockey player," I began. "You could make millions of dollars, and date Anna Kournikova. Though she would be a bit of a cougar by then."

"I saw a cougar at the zoo, Daddy!"

"Oh, trust me, they're everywhere, kid. Anyway, let's see... draft year 2017... Yup, the lockout should be just about over by then."

"What's a lockout, Daddy? Isn't that what Mom did to you last week when you went out with the boys, got home three hours late and tripped over the dog?"

"Uh... something like that. OK, how about a basketball player? You could have a Hummer and a shoe deal before you finish high school! But to be an NBA player, son, you have to have a good vertical. And a great lawyer."

"Dad, what's a verti..."

"Don't worry about it, buddy. Truth is, I'm barely 5-foot-10. Your Mom is 5-foot-3 in pumps. And neither one of us has much of a crossover, so the Lakers are probably out of the question. The Clippers, on the other hand..."

He was getting fidgety. I hadn't struck a chord yet.

"Maybe you should be a pro golfer. No height required there! You could wear funky slacks and date Swedish nannies!"

"Awesome! Can I make the little ball go sideways and hit the lady next to us like you did at the driving range?"

"Look, kid, I told you. Range balls are inconsistent. And you know I don't like hitting off mats, so back off. Wait! I got it! How about football! You could get a full scholarship to a Top 20 Program, get $1,000 a week allowance from some sleazy booster, and get drafted first overall by Buffa... Oh God, No! No! Please don't ever play football, son! I couldn't put you through that Hell. Why don't you focus on baseball?"

"But, Dad, I can't catch."

"You don't need to, son. That's why they have the DH! We'll get you A-Rod money! You can be just like all the sluggers today, buying all sorts of fancy cars, bling and designer... uh... steroids. OK, maybe that's not such a great idea either."

He looked discouraged.

"Hey, maybe you could be an agent, son. Earn 5 per cent of everything your clients make without ever taking a hit!"

"Would I still make a lot of money being one of those, Daddy?"

"As long as Glen Sather is still around."

He still didn't look sold.

"Why don't you become a broadcaster, buddy. Just like Daddy! Broadcasters are the true heroes of sport. They dedicate their lives to bringing the public the games they love, and the information they need. It takes courage, strength and integrity. Now that would be a noble profession for you."

"A sportscaster! Neat! Do I get a powder puff like you, Daddy? Remember when you cried when you couldn't find yours?"

"I told you that never leaves this house."

Right about then, I figured I should control my inner-psychosportsdad, and try to do the right thing.

"The truth is, son, you can be whatever you want to be when you grow up, even..."

(Swallowing hard.)

"... if it isn't in sports. Money, women, bling... those things aren't important. I'll love you and support you no matter what career path you choose."

I put my arm around him, and we sat quietly for a while. Pure Hallmark.

"So, buddy, what *do* you want to be when you grow up?"

He thought about it long and hard.

"I'm not sure, yet. Either a Transformer or a dinosaur."

(Sigh.)

• • •

Postscript: He's 10 now, and still contemplating all career options, though I believe he's realized dinosaur is a long shot. And just to be clear, that story about the powder puff: I didn't really cry, OK? I welled up a bit, but there were no tears.

JUST (DON'T) DO IT!

June 2002

Apologies, Nike. We've had to alter your slogan for the upcoming World Cup of Soccer.

Seems Italian manager Giovanni Trapattoni has banned his players from, umm... geez... golly, how do I... you know... the world's most popular coed sport (here's a hint: it ain't badminton).

"To achieve certain results, you have to set some rules for yourselves," says Trapattoni.

So the only lovin' his players will get is from cheering fans (and each other in the post-goal celebrations, where they often reach third base).

It's the ultimate red card. No more moaning. No more writhing. No more screaming. Except, of course, after diving to try to draw a foul.

The pre-tournament nookie-ban is apparently commonplace in soccer. No wonder they peel off their shirts after they score. Gotta get naked sometime.

Truth is, this is hardly new. For centuries, coaches have been cranky on the hanky-panky, fearing their players will wear themselves out, or perhaps pull something (insert your own lame joke).

Absence makes the heart grow fonder. Abstinence makes the team grow stronger.

Or not. There actually have been detailed scientific studies on the effect sex has on athletic performance.

Lab Rat: "You want us to do what before we go through the maze? Yeee-haaaaa! Cruelty to animals my a--! This is Ratopia!"

Uh, actually, the tests were on humans.

Lab Rat: "Damn you, humans! All I do is give, give, give. You shoot diseases into my butt, you take out pieces of my brain, and when I have a chance to get a little tail, you suddenly decide to use your own monkeys. I'm calling PETA!"

In 1995, a research team took a group of physically fit men, and looked at the effect of sexual intercourse 12 hours before a strenuous workout on a treadmill. It found there was no difference in the performance (the treadmill performance, silly) of those who did and those who didn't. Except maybe for the incessant hooting and high-fiving among the one group.

In a similar Swiss study reported in the *Journal of Sports Medicine and Physical Fitness* (I actually giggled after writing that. I have now officially done more research on this than on any term paper in four years of university. I may sell it on the Internet as a thesis.), a group comprised of weightlifters, endurance athletes and team-sport players worked out once after having sex, and once without. There was no difference in their results either, except for the subjects who had intercourse within two hours of the test. They took longer to get their heart rate down after the workout.

"See, honey, a two-hour recovery time is normal!"

In fact, some research has shown that sex may actually *improve* athletic performance (which would instantly explain the long, great career of one Wilt Chamberlain).

A survey of London marathon runners found that those who had sex the night before the race had faster finishing times than those who didn't. It also marked the first time in sexual history that anyone had bragged about getting done quicker.

Apparently, during sex, endorphins and serotonin are released *(this is so romantic)*, and those chemicals produce a natural high, which, some experts say, can dull pain, and perhaps even provide a second wind, thus boosting athletic performance.

A prominent female researcher did an extended study involving NBA players. But we're still waiting for Madonna to publish her results.

As for Team Italia's ban, it extends through the first round, after which wives and girlfriends will be allowed to "visit," but Trapattoni has told players to use "moderation." Which, for sex-starved Italian footballers, will likely be about seven hours a day. But as long as it's wives and girlfriends, the Italians should be just fine. As Casey Stengel once said: "The trouble is not that players have sex the night before a game. It's that they stay out all night looking for it."

On a final, personal note, I, too, have abstained for the duration of several World Cups.

Just never on purpose.

• • •

Postscript: Italy had, by their standards, a disastrous World Cup in 2002. They barely survived the first round, and then were knocked out by South Korea in round two. Conclusion: the lack of sexual relations clearly affected the team's productivity. I cite this example to my wife every time she asks me to do yardwork.

THE BIG HURT

March 2002

So what is the world's roughest sport?

The game of life, apparently. Our beloved athletes are going down in bunches! They are spraining, straining, tearing and breaking. And that's just on off-days.

It's a dangerous world out there. Just ask Colleen Jones, Canada's women's curling champ, whose status for the Worlds is in jeopardy after she injured her neck. She suspects it may have happened while she was, gulp, getting her hair braided.

Yikes. Who's her stylist, Bryan Marchment?

Braiding her hair?!? No wonder we haven't heard from Bo Derek in years. She's probably in long-term physiotherapy.

Many other jocks have DL'd themselves. Take Kansas City Royals outfielder Mark Quinn, who will miss the start of the baseball season after cracking a rib kung fu fighting. Good glove. Good bat. Bad Ninja.

At least Chow Yun Quinn owned up. San Francisco infielder Jeff Kent said he broke his wrist washing his truck. Strange how all these eyewitnesses saw him wipe out popping wheelies on his motorcycle, a no-no in his contract. Bad lie, Jeff. No one believes a major leaguer would wash his own vehicle.

Perhaps they shouldn't open their own boxes either, as San Diego pitcher Adam Eaton found out when he stabbed himself trying to open a DVD package (hope those 12 minutes of extra footage were good).

Pitchers should keep their cutting to fastballs. The Legend of Bobby Ojeda and the Hedge-Trimmer from Hell should be required reading for all rookies (Bobby trimmed all right, trimmed off the top of his finger and missed the last month of a season).

Ball players leading the sporting world in RBIs: Really Bizarro Injuries. Poor Vince Coleman had his leg eaten by a tarp rolling machine and missed the '85 Series (a scene eerily reminiscent of Quint getting swallowed by the shark in *Jaws*). Pitcher Steve Foster got so worked up watching a motivational speaker rip a phonebook in half; he had to try it himself. Dislocated shoulder.

"I am a good person! I can succeed! I will succ... AHHHHGGGGGG!"

Brian Giles went down with spider bites. This may explain Glenallen Hill's arachnophobic nightmare, causing him to fall through a glass table and miss a bunch of games. Outfielder Jose Cardinal couldn't sleep at all because he said he heard crickets chirping in his hotel room. Scratched. Sammy Sosa and Russ Davis both slept well, but on the wrong shoulder. Out of the lineup.

Right shoulder, wrong eye for Chris Brown, who strained an eyelid sleeping. How exactly do you rehab from that?

Personal Trainer: "C'mon, Brown! Gimme three more winks! Three more, you wuss!"

Hope he was careful with the A535. Hope Ken Griffey was, too. He missed a game after his protective cup slipped and pinched one of Junior's... juniors.

It's enough to make you puke, which Kevin Mitchell once did, straining a muscle in the process. Maybe it was bad fish. Oh sorry, that was Mark Portugal who missed a start after getting food poisoning from eating some nasty mahi-mahi. Should have had the carp, which is what English soccer keeper David Seaman was planning on doing until he wrecked his shoulder trying to reel in a big one. Almost ended his career. So Seaman decided he should stick to watching TV in his leisure time. Until he broke a bone reaching for his remote.

Don't feel too silly, Dave. Another soccer player, Robbie Keane, tore his knee cartilage making the same move. Damn that *Coronation Street!*

Where will the carnage end?

At least athletes who hurt themselves playing other sports can maintain some sense of dignity. Unless, of course, it's New Orleans Saints tight end Cam Cleeland, who tore his Achilles tendon playing golf.

Golfers should be hurt playing football. Football players should not be hurt playing golf. Maybe they just need to train harder. That's what Moises Alou was doing... when he fell off his treadmill and tore up his knee. It had almost healed when he ran over his son on his bike, and re-injured it. He was out almost a year. Moises should seriously consider becoming a Bubble Boy.

Geez, maybe the safest place for our athletes is the field of play. If they make it out there. Philadelphia Eagles defensive tackle Hollis Thomas broke his foot against the Giants this past season... in the pre-game introductions.

I guess those who somehow make it to game-time healthy should celebrate. Just not like Cardinals kicker Bill Gramatica, who tore up his knee jumping up and down after a field goal. Season over. Or French soccer hero Thierry Henry, who ran to the corner of the field after a goal, and smacked himself in the face with the flagstick. Stitches. Maybe they should just stick to high-fives. Then again, former Brave Terry Harper threw out his shoulder giving his teammate one. DL.

And you thought their egos were fragile.

As for Colleen Jones and her painful 'do, she'll suck it up. This is curling, remember. It's not the Ultimate Fighting Finals. But a valuable lesson has been learned. When it comes to hairstyling, curlers should just stick to... curlers.

• • •

Postscript: *This column really should have become required reading for professional athletes, especially baseball players. Like Milton Bradley, who tore up his knee arguing with an umpire. Or pitcher Joel Zumaya, who hurt his wrist playing Guitar Hero. Or fellow pitcher Terry Mulholland, who scratched his right eye by rolling over a loose feather in a hotel pillow. Or Clint Barmes, a National League Rookie of the Year front-runner in 2008, until he broke his left collarbone carrying deer meat up the stairs. Or Smoltz, who scalded himself while ironing a shirt. While he was wearing it.*

MATS, PLEASE PUT US OUT OF OUR MISERY

December 2008

My least favourite season in this business, my *annus horribilis*, was 2004–05, a.k.a, the NHL Lockout. Not only was there no hockey, but months went by without anything of substance happening, yet we still had to talk about it on TV every night. It became *Seinfeld*, without the comedy. A show about nothing.

Mats Sundin has become The Lockout, version 2K8.

For six months, we've been waiting for him to make up his mind. Six months!?! Presidents and prime ministers have been elected. Economies have crumbled. And still, we wait on Mats. Somebody shoot me. Wait, time to update that phrase: Somebody Plaxico Burress me.

In what psychologists would deem a cry for help, I decided to compile a timeline of the Sundin saga, a form of self-inflicted torture much more horrific than anything that sicko in the *Saw* movies could dream up. I've added footnotes for… umm… historical perspective.

June 12–Toronto grants permission to the New York Rangers to talk to Sundin. (Doesn't that feel like it was 27 years ago?)

June 20–Leafs grant Montreal permission to talk to Sundin. (Wouldn't life be great if people couldn't talk to you unless they were granted permission? Like, say... telemarketers. And in-laws.)

July 1–Sundin officially becomes a free agent. (Within hours, Michael Ryder gets $4 million a year, Jeff Finger gets $3.5 million a year, Cristobal Huet gets $5.6 million. What does that makes Mats worth? This is going to get silly.)

July 1–Vancouver offers Sundin $20 million over two years. (Told ya.)

July 10–Sundin says no thank you to Vancouver, and all other offers, saying he's not sure if he wants to play. (When you can say no to $20 million, you clearly have made way too much money in your life. Or you really, really, hate rain.)

July 15–Rangers officially declare they're still interested. (I officially declare that I'm losing interest already.)

July 23–Report indicates Sundin will decide his future on Aug. 1. (I recoil in fear, thinking TSN will schedule a "Sundin Decision Day" special, forcing me to miss August long weekend horseshoe tournament at cottage. This would hurt me more than you will ever know.)

July 30–Sundin's agent JP Barry says on Vancouver radio that six teams are interested in Sundin and that he's informed them he'll make a decision in August. (I believe this is the same way Tom Cruise chooses his wives.)

Aug. 1–Sundin sets soft deadline of Aug. 15 for decision. ("Soft deadline"? Isn't that like "almost pregnant"?)

Sept. 2–Sundin announces that he won't make his decision until after the season starts. (So when you said "soft deadline," you meant really really soft, like... mushed bananas.)

Sept. 3–Sundin says: "I haven't even looked at different options, or teams, or where to play. My first question is, do I want to play any more?" (13 seasons with the Leafs can have that effect on a guy.)

Sept. 5–Sundin returns to Toronto to play in a charity ball-hockey game. (Confused New York Islanders scout notes that his skating looks shaky.)

Sept. 5–Sundin meets with Cliff Fletcher. (Jokester Sundin tells Fletcher he's now ready to waive his no-trade clause. Cliff doesn't laugh.)

1985–Austrian rock singer Falco records "Rock Me Amadeus!" (Sorry, mind drifted off for a minute.)

Oct. 4–Senators owner Eugene Melynk woos Sundin during "chance" meeting at Sens-Pens game in Sweden. (And by "chance meeting," we mean Melnyk hid in a storage closet in Sundin's luxury box for 18 hours until he showed up.)

Oct. 30–Sundin starts training in LA. (... To be a contestant on *American Gladiators.*)

Nov. 3–Bryan Murray indicates Ottawa is still interested in Sundin. (And by "interested," he means, "Choose us! Choose us! Oh please please please! Have you looked at our secondary scoring?!? We're dying here, Mats!" I'm paraphrasing.)

Nov. 4–Sundin meets with Brian Burke in Anaheim. (To do what? Help him pack?)

Nov. 19–Sundin meets with Bob Gainey in Los Angeles. (No one gets more free lunches than Mats.)

Nov. 21–Sundin meets with Melnyk in Los Angeles. (Why didn't Mats just have one of those group dates they do on *The Bachelor*?)

Dec. 8–Sundin sets "target date" of Dec. 15 to make decision. (Is it just me, or does "target date" sound an awful lot like "soft deadline"?)

Dec. 14–Sundin talks with the New York Rangers. (Hey, wait a second. We did that one June 12! Is this show running on a loop?)

Dec. 12–Dejected columnist realizes he has spent half a day researching a story he was sick of five months ago. Sticks pen in eye.

• • •

Postscript: Sundin signed with Vancouver in late December 2008. He was a non-factor most of his half-season there. The following year threatened to be a sequel to the painful Mats-athon. But just before the season started, he announced his retirement in Sweden, saving us all several more months of pain and suffering. Sundin had a terrific career, and is probably a Hall-of-Famer. But he probably should have retired as a Maple Leaf, one season earlier.

AU REVOIR EXPOS

September 2005

I just heard that an old friend passed away. Not to sound cold, but I didn't get emotional. After all, I hadn't gone to see him in years. In fact, no one had seen much of him of late. He hadn't moved or anything, he was still around. People just left him alone. There was a time though when he was The Man. We'd drive two hours every weekend to visit his home. He'd dance and goof around with the kids. Everybody loved the big fella.

Yup, sure gonna miss you, Youppi.

OK, so I don't do sucky well. Even if I did, it would be wrong to get all Dick Vermeil about a team I hadn't seen in person in seven years, and watched on TV about as often as *Dr. Phil.*

The only ones who truly have a right to get mushy over the Montreal Expos' demise are the employees who'll lose their jobs, the couple thousand fans who've stuck with them over the years and, of course, that big orange furry ball of love himself, the Youpster.

The rest of us didn't care enough before, so we don't have the right to say we care now.

But we can remember. Remember a time when we did care.

I'll remember the mid-'70s, listening to the Expos in French on my AM radio in Ottawa, which in baseball terms, was a suburb of Montreal. And though I understood enough to follow along, there were some slight problems.

Namely the mysterious "Orling," a player I could never find in the box scores, but who seemed to dominate the game on the radio. It seemed every second hit went in his direction: *"Balle frappe Orling."* It took me about a half-season to figure out Orling was actually *"Hors ligne,"* translation: foul. I sheepishly scratched the number 24 ORLING jersey off my birthday list.

I'll remember finally getting Duke and Dave (Snider and Van Horne) on English radio. They were jock-Mozart. I'd waste away night after summer night listening to them while tossing a beat-up Slazenger against the aluminum siding of my house, trying to make Ozzie Smith diving grabs into the hedge.

I'll remember spending one of my first dates ever listening to a game at a movie (I think it was *Zapped!* with Scott Baio and Willie Aames, so you could pretty much follow without the audio). I guarantee she doesn't remember that. Or me.

I'll remember walking into that stadium and smelling burnt rubber, only to realize it was the hotdogs. The Big Owe weenie didn't even have a bun, just a piece of semi-toasted soggy bread that only stretched around half of it. It looked like a Britney Spears outfit, there was so much meat exposed. And yet, I still ate three a game. C'mon, it's baseball!

I'll remember being there the night they booed Jeff Reardon's wife. She was introduced between games of a double-header in recognition of some charity work. Problem was, hubby had blown the save in game one. Tough crowd.

I'll remember my 16th birthday, when my sisters baked me Tim Raines head. Not a decapitated Gwyneth-Paltrow-at-the-end-of-Se7en head, but a cake. It was a darn good likeness, too, complete with an Expos ballcap. A couple of my friends took icing sugar and sprinkled it under his nose for the mandatory Tim Raines coke joke. Not funny. I worshipped Tim Raines.

I'll remember rewriting the entire lyrics to "I Don't Like Mondays" on the fateful day in '81. This, after Rick Monday's home run and Jerry White's subsequent first pitch meager game-ending ground ball after two straight walks in the bottom of the ninth. Last few lines (with sincere apologies to Bob Geldof):

'Cause Jerry's first ball hitting, and Lopes is mitting, and the final out has now been made. And I can see no reasons, cause there are no reasons, why the Series should even be played. Oh, oh, oh, oh, oh. Tell me why. I don't like Monday. Tell me why. I don't like Monday. Tell me why. I don't like Monday. I want to sho-oo-oo-oo-oo-ooot Rick Mon-day down.

What do you want…. I was 14.

I'll remember taking a glove to every single game, even when I was too old for it to be cool, desperate to catch one foul ball. One night, I went to get a rubber weenie, and was strolling towards my section when the Cardinals' George Hendricks looped one in that direction. Seconds later, there was my buddy on the big screen, gleaming like he'd just caught the freakin' Hope Diamond.

The ball had bounced off my seat, and into his hands.

I won't remember '94. That traumatic memory has been suppressed, and will likely only come out about 20 years from now in therapy.

I dug through some boxes in the basement the other day, searching for Expos mementos. All I came up with was a wrapper from a "Cro-Bar," the Warren Cromartie-inspired, and oh-so-tasty, answer to the Baby Ruth candy bar.

One lousy souvenir. But *beaucoup de souvenirs*, as they say in Moe-Ray-Al.

And those cannot be shipped to DC.

• • •

Postscript: *The Montreal Expos became the Washington Nationals in 2005. They have yet to have a winning season in Washington.*

KERRY FRASER'S HAIR SCARE

November 2006

I have seen the Eighth Wonder of the World. Up close.

I have watched it. Studied it. Even touched it. I spent an entire day in its presence. It is mystical, magical, unexplainable. And most of all, immovable.

It is Kerry Fraser's lid.

For more than three decades, Fraser's coif has been astonishing fans in hockey arenas across North America. He hears the whispers everywhere he goes.

"Is it real?"

"How does it stay like that?"

"That was !#*@!NG high-sticking you A*&@%!" (OK, that last one likely doesn't have anything to do with the hair. Likely wasn't a whisper either.)

Well, if I may paraphrase Teri Hatcher (referring to a different body part on *Seinfeld*): it is real, and it's spectacular. And it is also about to be hidden away. Buried beneath a helmet.

This, my friends, is a tragedy.

Sure, making helmets mandatory for referees is wise and, frankly, long overdue. But hiding a hockey treasure like Fraser's hair? That's akin to keeping the Mona Lisa in the closet at the Louvre.

Or worse. We have seen what helmets do to hair. Messing it. Flattening it. And sometimes it seems, rubbing it right off, leading to hockey's most horrific mutation: the receding mullet. Al Iafrate anyone? (Completely unrelated Al Iafrate anecdote: He appeared as a guest on our show two years ago. He rode his Harley into the studio, wearing a sweat suit. We set up a radar gun on our fake rink (RIP), and he took a shot from a small wooden riser, with zero room to step into it, and hit 99 mph. One take. In flip-flops. Ridiculous.)

Two months into the season, we are still waiting to see Fraser's Helmethead debut. Back in September, he was helping his daughter move, and dropped a TV on his big toe, shattering it. (Too bad. I'm convinced if he dropped it on his head, it would have bounced off that lid like a beach ball. It's impenetrable. NASA really needs to take some samples.)

Rehab complete, he will finally don the bucket Thursday as Tampa visits Boston. As that terrifying night closed in, we went to visit him at his home near Philadelphia to see how he is coping with the impending end of his perfect 'do.

We found him quivering in the corner like a wet puppy. OK, not really. But he acted that way brilliantly in an *NHL on TSN* sketch we were taping about Fraser's supposed fear of Helmethead.

Seriously, we've shot a bunch of shtick pieces over the years, and never had a more eager leading man. He picked us up at the airport, let us stay at his house, cooked us breakfast and chauffeured us all over Philly while we made him do ridiculous stunts while wearing a hockey helmet. Let's see Philip Seymour Hoffman do that!

But the star was the hair. No matter what we did, it wouldn't budge.

We made him wear the helmet as he ran up and down the Rocky steps a half dozen times. When the helmet came off, the hair was perfect. He wore it through a workout in the gym. Stayed perfect. He skated for an hour with it on. Perfect. And when we finally soaked it and used half a jar of some paste or grooming cream to make it look bad for a dream sequence shot, he ran his fingers through it once and it bounced back up like a freakin' Weeble.

So he will undoubtedly triumph over Helmethead. In fact, Fraser's hair may be the single greatest genetic gift I've ever seen. Next to Eva Longoria.

• • •

Postscript: Fraser took the helmet off for good after the 2009–10 NHL season, retiring after more than 37 years as an NHL official. He refereed more than 1,900 regular season games, the most in history. Both the man, and the coif, are likely headed for the Hockey Hall of Fame.

TV ECSTASY

These are the three moments that changed my life:

1. When, after dressing as Run from Run-DMC, and rapping a Shakespearean sonnet for a Grade 12 English oral mid-term, my teacher exploded: "You, son, are an idiot. And you should go work in TV because that's where all idiots end up."

2. When, while waiting in line outside a bar on a frigid January night in Ottawa, this impossibly hot blonde tapped me on the shoulder and asked me if she could borrow my gloves. To show her gratitude, she bore my three children. A little excessive maybe, but I'm not complaining.

3. When I bought my PVR.

Not necessarily in that order.

You know how people always say, "How did we ever survive without the Internet?" Or bank cards, or cellphones, or... *Maxim*. Well, that's the way I feel about my Personal Video Recorder. (Aside:

PVR is the name given by Bell to its digital recording product. You may also know it as TiVo, or some other brand name given by your respective cable or satellite provider. Despite the fact this writer works for a company owned by Bell, he has not received any complimentary equipment for his endorsement. Which, by the way, is a crock. You think he'd get a dish, or a phone, or free Internet, or something. Nope. Jack-Squat. Not even a T-shirt. He got more swag when he worked at Ponderosa in the '80s. At least they let him eat the leftover Jell-O.)

Where was I? Oh yeah, PVR. The greatest development in video since *Girls Gone Wild*. If you don't have it, or you don't know what it is, you're a TV caveman. You're probably in a loincloth trying to make fire as we speak. Seriously, you might as well still have beta.

PVR makes you God of your TV. You can pause live shows, rewind (I believe the Janet Jackson wardrobe malfunction was the moment PVR officially arrived: "Dude, was that her boob?!?"—rewind—"Holy crap, it was!"), and record things off TV with the push of one little red button. No tapes. No poor-quality playback grainier than the lunar landing (the first one). No timers more complex than logarithms. The PVR is Fisher-Price easy.

And that's only half of it. You can fly through commercials and pre-game shows and intermissions at 300x speed. (Wait. Uhh. Oh-Oh. Forget I said that.) For a sports fan, this is the best invention since cheerleaders. You can watch games in a fraction of the time. Anytime!

Back in January, my kids had two birthday parties to attend on the day of the NFC and AFC Championship Games (not enough parents take into account future playoff schedules when they conceive… so selfish). So I PVR'd 'em. In the seven hours I would have spent in front of the TV watching the games live, I instead:

• Made both parties

• Took down the Christmas lights

• Worked out (jazzercise, as always)

• Made dinner

- Did the dishes

- Bathed the kids

- Walked the dog

- Seduced the wife… twice

- Watched both games in two hours flat.

(OK, I made up that one part just to sound impressive. Truth is, I never make dinner.)

This past weekend alone, I PVR'd *SportsCenter*, three college basketball games, Dave Hodge's show, the end of the golf tournament and *Kangaroo Jack*. (I did that one for the kids, until I saw Estella Warren. I owe an apology to Jerry O'Connell. He was my favourite punch line when I heard he was in a movie with a talking marsupial. No one mentioned the make-out scenes with Estella. I now believe Jerry O'Connell is the pre-eminent actor of our generation.)

Nothing PVRs better than golf. You can record an entire final round and watch it in about a half-hour. Golf is actually much more entertaining at 15x speed. Even Bernhard Langer plays fast. And it's not like you miss much without the commentary.

Roger Maltbie: "That's a good-looking shot."

Dan Hicks: "Nicely done."

Johnny Miller: "I was better."

One warning. PVR is a TV viewer's crack. You cannot stop. You end up recording stuff you'd never watch normally.

"Hey, look! There's an all-new *Hope & Faith* on tonight!"

And I can no longer watch live TV. It's too darn slow! If I want to watch something at 8:00, I'll sit around until 8:30, just so I can PVR and skip the commercials. There's no sadder moment in a PVRer's life than hitting the fast-forward button during an ad, and getting the "LIVE" message. It's crushing.

PVR doesn't just make TV better. It makes you a better person. Remember this?

Her: "Honey… don't forget tonight we're going to look at lamp-shades!"

You: "But what about the footba…"
Her: "You promised!"
You (defeated): All right, Schmoofie."
Now it's:
You: "No problem, babe. Just let me set the PVR!"
Her: "Sorry, hun… already set for *Desperate Housewives!*"
OK, so it's not perfect.

• • •

Postscript: *The new PVRs make my original look like an 8-track. They can record two things at once, and have a gazillion hours of storage space. If I end up in a coma, or prison, or something, I have already instructed my children to tape all hockey and football games, plus every episode of* SportsCenter, Dexter, Entourage, Californication, Curb Your Enthusiasm, The Amazing Race *and* The Bachelor *(we all have our skeletons).*

GOLDEN SUNDAY

February 2002

Son, I'm not sure when I'll let you read this.

Maybe in 2010 when you're 10, and we're watching the Olympics together. Maybe when you're 18 or so, and really starting to understand passion and patriotism. Maybe another 15 or 20 years beyond that, when you have your own kids and start to get all sucky and emotional like your Dad. Maybe it'll just be the first time you ask me what "That Day" was really like, and you look at me like you really want to know. Or maybe your little sister will ask me first. That'd be cool, too. Or maybe I'm just doing this for myself, so I'll never forget the feeling.

It doesn't really matter.

The thing is, someday, somewhere, someone will ask you where you were when Canada won Gold in 2002. And instead of saying, "I was only two, I don't remember," you can tell them this:

Your father was a wreck all morning. Pacing like the night you were born. Thankfully, I found John Cusack back-to-back classics on MoviePix to kill the agonizing wait.

First up, *Say Anything*, featuring one of the best movie scenes of all-time, when Lloyd Dobler stands outside his girlfriend's house, holding a ghetto blaster over his head playing Peter Gabriel's "Your Eyes" (their song) after she dumped him. I instantly ponder running out on to the street, holding a ghetto blaster high above my head, and blasting "O Canada".

Next up, *The Sure Thing*. Just the title was a good omen, I figured. We all search for omens on a day like this. And there were more to come.

Around lunch, you come running back in from the grocery store with your Mom, carrying some special gold coin they were giving out with a carton of Coke. It was a Team Canada promotion, with a Scott Niedermayer likeness on it. Most days, I'd chuck it in a drawer. But on this day, I delicately place it on the mantle like it was your Great Grandpa's ashes or something, then decide it belongs on the TV, so it may transmit good vibes to Salt Lake in some weird poltergeist kind of way. (In the history books, you'll read about the famous Loonie buried in the ice. In our family, the legend will be the Niedermayer Coke Coin on top of the Sony.)

When you wake up from your nap just before game time, I let you pick out a clean shirt. (Son, you have an unhealthy obsession with clothes for a two-year-old boy. Your Mother thinks it's cute. I'm somewhat concerned.) When you point to your red Roots sweatshirt with Canada on the front, I almost begin to weep. You never pick that shirt. This is too good!

By game time, all the neighbours are over, 20 strong, and you're nowhere to be seen. Off in the playroom, oblivious to your Father's impending ulcer.

Son, it was awesome. I'll spare you most of the play-by-play, because I've saved you the tape. Maybe you can watch it the same day you read this (although I'm guessing VCRs are probably the 8-track tapes of your generation, so you may be screwed).

We reacted like we'd won the lottery with every Team Canada goal, and lost a loved one with every near miss. (When Mario missed an open net, I believe I performed an exact recreation of Willem

Dafoe's death scene in *Platoon*, when he gets shot about 50 times in the back, throws his arms in the air and then falls face-forward to the ground in super slo-mo.)

There is one image I'll never forget. The Great One (that guy I told you about so many times), after the outcome was clear and the world was lifted off his shoulders, gazing down towards the ice, pumping his fist and yelling a distinctly Canadian phrase that any amateur lip-reader couldn't possibly miss: "F----n' Eh!" Your Grandma won't be happy with me, and I'll probably have to yell at you if you repeat it (unless you're, like, 32 now), but trust me, at that moment, it was Shakespeare.

You see, right or wrong, we'd always been known as this polite, conservative, insecure nation. The US's timid little brother. And 50 years without a gold in Our Game didn't help the fragile ego. We needed to kick some ass for once. And on that day, we did.

With three minutes left, I came and pulled you out of the play-room. You came reluctantly I might add. If you had your choice you would have spent the greatest sports moment of my generation doing a Franklin the Turtle puzzle. I sat you on my lap on the floor. Even if you had no chance to remember it, I wanted you to be able to tell your friends you did watch it.

I even stuck the video camera on top of the TV, shooting back at us for our reaction. Upon reviewing it later, I realized that when Sakic scored, I leapt up and almost pile-drove you into the hardwood. Sorry.

We shouted down from 10, and you just looked around, giving us your patented "I believe these people are aliens" stare.

And then it was over.

And neighbours jumped on furniture, hugged and sang "O Canada". And you ran around the room high-fiving every single one of us. And it was the same scene in just about every family room in the country.

Downtown (every Canadian city's downtown), they rushed out of the bars and ran, and screamed, and honked, and sang, and cried, and leapt into the arms of strangers, and hung out of car windows, and shut down major arteries, and played street hockey until the wee hours of Monday.

I thought more than once about jumping in the car and joining them. Instead, I just sat on the floor with you, paralyzed with glee, watching the Canadian players holding their kids, letting them play with their Gold Medals as if they were some cheesy coins they'd gotten out of a carton of Coke.

Afterwards, when everyone had gone home, you sat on my lap, and we watched the endless shots of people cheering from coast to coast. Then all of a sudden you pointed at the screen, and blurted out one of the newest words in your tiny, but ever-expanding, vocabulary.

"Happ... eeee!"

Son, you have no idea.

• • •

Postscript: I wrote this column in a hazy blur at two in the morning after Canada's gold medal win. At the time, it felt like a once-in-a-lifetime moment. It was our generation's 1972. That is, until Vancouver, 2010, came along, and blew the 2002 moment away. My guess is that 30 years from now, everyone will remember where they were when Crosby scored to win gold in Vancouver. And the 2002 gold will become an afterthought. It just didn't have that one defining goal that Crosby gave us, or Paul Henderson before him.

But 2002 will remain special to me, because I got to watch it as a fan, with my boy and baby daughter with me. I couldn't be there when they watched the 2010 game at home with Mom, their baby sister, and half my son's hockey team. Dad was stuck at work. Of course, his workplace was 30 feet away from where Crosby scored. So he wasn't complaining.

COLLATERAL DAMAGE

May 2005. (The full NHL season has been lost to the lockout. Commissioner Gary Bettman and NHL Players' Association head Bob Goodenow continue to meet, with little progress.)

• • •

Hey, Bob, Gary! Got a minute? Before you get together this week to make "no significant progress," I was wondering if you could drop by my neighbourhood? I've got some pals I'd like you to meet.

See over there, just up the street from my place? Those are the Hilliard boys, Chris and Mark, two brothers (14 and 16) who are sports freaks. So are their buddies, Jeff, Travis, Braden, Kevin, Dylan, David and Paul. For the last few springs, they've had the best street hockey game in the hood (OK, hood is a stretch for our little suburban Pleasantville, but I feel it gives me street cred). Every day after school, they'd be there. They didn't even have to call each other. Just show up with a stick at 4:00 and it was, "Game on!"

Now, look over here behind my house. This is where the younger kids hang. Hey! There's my next-door neighbour, Cameron. He plays

Atom AA and can Al MacInnis a tennis ball top shelf. He almost Van Goghed my ear last spring. And those are the twins, Reid and Connor. Don't ask me which is which, but they're both relentless on the forecheck. Oh, and the kid playing with my son is Calvin, the prodigy. I never saw Sidney Crosby at four, but I reckon he was a lot like Calvin. Can you be considered a legitimate prospect when you still wear Gymboree?

You see, our back lane is street-hockey heaven. It's a new development, so the pavement is fresh and there's almost no traffic. You could play three hours without yelling "Car!" once. We had one game last year with 14 kids, all in different NHL jerseys. It was like a freakin' Starter ad.

But here's the thing, Bob and Gary. Look at what they're doing now! They're playing basketball. And they're skateboarding. And they're... dismembering their sister's Dora the Explorer doll with a golf club... "HEY, CUT THAT OUT!" (Sorry, my boy has issues.)

Point is, there's not a stick in sight. I haven't seen one all spring.

"Hmm, I think we played once," Chris Hilliard says after careful thought. "I think."

"We're just not into it," adds brother Mark. "When there's no playoffs on TV, you just don't feel like playing. So we shoot hoops. Or play poker" (which is a whole other column).

I try to go all Mike Wallace on Cameron, the eight-year-old next door, as he launches brick after gleeful brick at the basket above his garage.

"C'mon, Cam, you love hockey? Why don't I ever see you play out here anymore?"

"Don't feel like it," he offers.

"Ever?"

"Nope."

And so his net sits leaned up against his back fence. In the exact spot we left it last fall. I think there's a nest in it.

Strange, isn't it, Gary and Bob? Sure, minor hockey did just fine this year without the NHL. It always will. But now that the seasons are over, now that the schedules have been ripped off the fridge, now that they have a choice what to do after school and on Saturday afternoon, they are leaving the sticks in the garage.

My boy, for one, doesn't get it. He's way too young to understand this lockout concept. I tried to explain it once and he responded (quoting word for word): "Can't somebody just give them a key?"

I don't even know if he realizes there wasn't a season. Still, from time to time, he asks me, "Why doesn't anyone want to play street hockey anymore?"

Maybe you'd like to answer him, Gary and Bob.

(Pause)

Didn't think so. Anyway, good luck with your meetings. Please, drop by anytime.

We'll shoot some hoops.

• • •

Postscript: The lockout ended two months later. Bob Goodenow stepped down soon after. The kids in my neighbourhood started playing street hockey again the next fall when the NHL came back, but never to the extent they did before. Give a child an excuse to find something else to do, and they will. I'm not sure Bob or Gary ever got that part.

HALF GOALTENDER, HALF ZOOLANDER

March 2007

I am standing in Ray Emery's closet, trying to figure out which of the dozen or so ridiculously expensive designer sunglasses he has spread meticulously across a shelf go best with the $4,000 suit he is letting me try on. (For the record, I usually buy my sunglasses at gas stations, and I wouldn't buy a $4,000 suit if it came with superpowers, so this is all a little foreign to me.)

It is a Senators' off-day long before Emery became one of THE stories of 2007 playoffs, both for his terrific play on the ice and for his poor alarm-clock-management and driving issues off it.

As he gives me a crash-course on his favourite colours and designers, I'm starting to feel like that fashion critic freak Cojo on *Entertainment Tonight*. (Editorial Note: Cojo is not to be confused with Cujo. Hmm. I wonder if that's ever happened? You know, some kid asks for an autographed Cujo jersey for Christmas, and his Mom gets confused and he ends up with a pink frilly man-blouse signed "Stay fabulous darling, luv, and wet kisses, Cojo." That could scar a kid for life.)

Emery is sick with a cold, and clearly dying to go to bed. He goes on at length about his love for the afternoon nap (which became abundantly clear last week when he slept in and missed his flight). Still, he patiently shows off every item in his wild wardrobe.

It features a rainbow of suits, some 50 pairs of shoes (including a pair of blue and yellow runners he calls his "Alfies"), a dozen watches (he should really set the alarm on every one), a club-hopping shirt for every day of the... century, and bling up the ying-ying. (I have no idea what that last part means, but it is extremely enjoyable to say aloud.)

"I used to live with him and I'd have to sleep on the couch because his clothes took up the entire other room," laughs Jason Spezza.

"He takes about three suitcases for a one-game road trip," adds road roommate Mike Comrie. "One time, he pulled this zebra blanket out of his suitcase. I didn't even want to ask what that was for."

C'mon, Mike. You were in the desert too long. Who doesn't accessorize with a zebra blanket these days? Brown is the new black, and zebra blanket is the new... uhh... scarf? Sweater? Gonch?

Emery does not know, nor care, whether his duds are cutting-edge fashion. He tells me over and over that he just wants "to be different."

Mission accomplished. His game-day arena arrivals have become the stuff of Sens legend. From the baby-blue suit and matching shoes ("Right out of the seventies" – Chris Kelly), to the black-and-white wide-pinstriped number ("My personal favourite... the Jailbird" – Wade Redden), which sometimes comes with a top hat.

The Razor's outlandish attire, and bad-boy behavior makes some (including, on occasion, teammates) roll their eyes and shake their heads. But perhaps, right here right now, he is exactly the personality the Senators need.

This team has always seemed too serious, too conservative. Their fragile confidence was written on their faces after a loss, and often, before one. When Ray Emery struts into the building in a wild purple suit, wearing that Cheshire-cat grin, it is so un-Ottawa-like, so un-Senator-like, you cannot help but think things have changed.

He is one different dude. This was the first hockey player interview I've done that had to be interrupted to feed a pet python a live mouse. I thought of that moment the other night watching the Senators dust off the Devils like a piece of lint on one of Emery's suits.

These Senators are looking more and more like the snake. And less and less like the mouse.

• • •

Postscript: *Emery led the Senators to the Stanley Cup Final that season, where they lost to Anaheim in five games. While his clothes stayed fresh, his act quickly grew old. The next season was a disaster, on and off the ice, for Emery. He showed up late for a practice and was sent home. He scrapped with one teammate, angered many others with his attitude and, worst of all, gave up too many goals. The Senators no longer wanted him, but couldn't trade him. So Emery went to Russia, where he behaved and played very well. He returned to the NHL in 2009 with the Philadelphia Flyers.*

HOW CANADA CAN
BOUNCE BACK

September 2000. (My first column for TSN, written during the Sydney Olympic Games, where Canadian athletes were struggling, except on the new Olympic sport of trampoline.)

• • •

OK, so we can no longer claim to have some of the best sprinters, cyclists, swimmers and rowers on the planet. But, man, can we bounce!

We have more kangaroo in us than the Aussies. We're human pogo sticks. Our team mascot should be Tigger. No wonder Pamela Anderson is a native daughter (who has more bounce than her?).

Forget the pool. Give up the track. We need to focus all our resources on the tramp. No, not Pam, silly. The tramp-OLINE! What? One obscure event is not enough to restore our damaged Olympic pride you say? Just wait.

If Dick Pound becomes the head of the International Olympic Committee, "The Next Juan," Canada will have serious IOC pull.

We'll just get Dick to add more bouncy events. Like rhythmic trampoline. And synchronized trampoline. (Aside: Do all events now have to be synchronized? And if they do synchronized sprinting, won't there always be an 8-way tie for first?) Why stop there? Platform trampoline. Ballroom trampoline. Equestrian trampoline *("Big Ben with a triple somersault, and still lands on his hooves!")*.

It will be our new national sport. The Walter Gretzkys of the next generation will dedicate their backyards to tramps. And when winter comes? No problem. High ceilings are in, anyway.

Start training your children now. We can no longer afford to bring our young athletes up the "Canadian" way: all soft and sweet. We need to be tough. German tough.

Crash!

"What was that, honey?"

"Oh, Billy just flew the hedge and landed in Mrs. Brown's azaleas."

"Dad! I need… paramedic."

"No, son. What you need is to GET BACK ON THE #*@!* TRAMPOLINE AND WORK ON YOUR DISMOUNT!"

Oh, and Mr. Pound, sir. While you're at it, we need to add another colour medal. Canadians finish fourth waaaay too often. I'm thinking pewter. Or maybe tin.

Brian Williams: "And so Canada completes its most successful Olympics ever: 1 Gold, 1 Silver, 5 Bronze and 23 Tin!

Tin and trampolines. Now that's a plan that can rally a nation.

Maybe when we're bouncing our way to tin after tin, we'll actually start supporting our athletes for more than two weeks every four years. And who knows? Maybe they'll actually get enough funding to train full-time AND live above the poverty line. *("Honey, wasn't that Curtis Myden working the drive-thru?")*

So, don't get down about our Olympic performance, Canada. Get up! And down! And up! And down! And up!

• • •

Postscript: *Dick Pound lost to Jacques Rogge in his bid to become IOC president, which hurt my trampolining campaign. Still, it has gone from the* *giggle-worthy novelty it was in 2000 to being one of Canada's best Olympic events. I thought I was joking about synchronized trampoline—until it became an actual sport shortly thereafter. Still waiting on equestrian trampoline—crossing my fingers for London, 2012.*

MR. KILREA'S OPUS

April 2009

Hmm, this is a problem.

How do you write an accurate Brian Kilrea tribute when all the good stories have too many expletives to repeat?

If they ever film "The Brian Kilrea Story," HBO will be the only option.

"I remember this one game we lost 7-2," says Brian Patafie, the 67's long-time athletic trainer. "I came home and my wife asked 'What did Killer say after the game?' I said, 'Do you want me to include all the expletives?' She said 'No.' So I said, 'He didn't say anything.'"

The punchline works because you know it's true. We just interviewed a dozen current and former Kilrea players for an upcoming piece on his retirement, and not one had a good yarn that could be told without editing to the point of distortion.

"There's nothing I can repeat on television," laughs Doug Wilson. And Michael Peca. And Gary Roberts. And Brian Campbell. And Nick Boynton. And Brendan Bell. And... all of them.

So instead, we turn to the serious stuff, the what-Killer-meant-to-me material. And sometimes the words wouldn't come easy here, either. For a different reason.

Take goalie-turned-analyst Darren Pang, one of the most cheerful, chatty characters you'll ever meet. This is a man who frequently makes monkey faces on national television (Panger does a monkey better than... most monkeys) just to crack up the host. He has also done his hilarious Kilrea imitation every single time I have worked with him, which is now in triple digits.

And yet, when we asked him to send a message to his old coach on camera, he lost it.

"Killer... I just can't say enough..." That's as far as Panger got before breaking down. And you know what? No more words were required.

Seeing Panger get that emotional, and hearing the countless other testimonials from Kilrea's former players this week, I keep thinking of *Mr. Holland's Opus*. I know, Killer isn't quite as warm and fuzzy as Richard Dreyfuss was in that tearjerker, about a music teacher who finally realizes how many lives he has touched.

But as you sit and read the alphabetical list of every player who has come through Killer's dressing room, 500 strong, you realize: they are Mr. Kilrea's Opus.

"I can remember when Steve Payne was with the team, and in his last year, we lost out in the playoffs in Peterborough," Kilrea remembers, sitting in the 67's empty dressing room.

"One of our guys came in and said, 'Steve's Dad wants to see you.' So I went out and he said, 'I just wanted to thank you. I gave you a boy and you are giving me back a man.'"

Killer's eyes well up. "That meant a lot."

And isn't that his true legacy? Sure, we'll all remember the two Memorial Cups and the countless quality NHL players he has developed. But in the end, it is the impact Kilrea has had on so many young lives that deserves the longest, and loudest, round of applause as he exits.

Just ask Lance Galbraith.

You won't see Lance on TSN talking about Killer. It's our nature to go to the big names for the quotes. But you'd be hard pressed to find a player Killer had a greater influence on.

Galbraith was a tough, talented hockey player coming out of bantam, but already had a well-earned rep of being a bad apple. Kilrea took a chance and drafted him anyway. But he almost never made it to Ottawa.

Galbraith had been arrested for stealing a car. Joyriding had overtaken hockey as his favourite hobby. He was likely headed for a juvenile detention centre. So, Kilrea found out who the presiding judge was in the case, and wrote him a letter.

"I guaranteed him that if he gave Lance a second chance, I would take care of him. I promised him the kid would leave here a better person."

Galbraith received a suspended sentence. He moved to Ottawa, in fact, right into Kilrea's house for a while, and became one of the most popular 67's of his era.

He is now 29, and still playing hockey, for the Alaska Aces of the ECHL. It's a life he loves. And one he is forever grateful for.

"I don't even like to think about what my life would have become if Killer didn't take that chance on me," says Galbraith. "He turned me around.

"He taught me about respect. Like how he always made us thank the restaurant owner or the cook after a meal. I always remembered that, and do it every time I eat somewhere. It was the little things like that. He made me a better person."

There you go. A great Killer story without a single expletive.

• • •

Postscript: I just finished writing a book with Killer called They Call Me Killer, *available at all reputable bookstores. (Sorry, that was pathetic and shameless.) I have been lucky enough to meet a lot of great characters in my 20-odd years in this business. Killer is my favourite. He is simply one of the funniest, most honest, loyal, tell-it-like-it-is, old-school hockey guys you will ever meet.*

THE BOY FROM
THE HOOD

December 2007

When it comes to hockey, Canada is the largest small town in the world. Chances are you know a guy who dates a girl who works with a dude whose sister-in-law's son played with Claude Giroux. Or Josh Godfrey. Or someone on Team Canada.

That's why I love the World Juniors. We all feel connected to the boys. Remember that movie game "Six Degrees of Kevin Bacon"? We get to do the same thing every year with Team Canada. Call it Six Degrees of Steve Mason. And when one of the kids actually comes from your hood, you get to adopt him.

"That's OUR boy!"

I know people in Orleans and Cumberland are doing it with Giroux. In Amherstview, outside of Kingston, the Godfrey family has welcomed several hundred new members.

And in my neck on the woods, everyone is gaga over our own local hero.

We live in Unionville, a community north of Toronto. It's a great little neighbourhood tucked in the middle of Markham, one of the fastest growing cities in Canada.

Not long after we moved here seven years ago, I started hearing stories about a skinny blond kid who was going to be The Next One. Or make that The Next Next One, since Crosby was already being dubbed The Next One back then (seems the shelf life on Next Ones is down to about two seasons).

For years, I couldn't get his name straight. Stavro? Stempo? Stamcoat? But the stories were grand.

By three, he was already a little Unionville celebrity. The families who went public skating every Saturday at the local rink would stare in amazement at the blond blur in the Leafs sweater who would whip around the ice like a squirrel on Red Bull.

At four, he signed up for house league. His first coach was Paul Titanic.

"He was mind-boggling," Titanic says with a chuckle. "Four years old and he was the best player in a league full of six-year-olds. By five, he had the skills of a 10-year-old. A good 10-year-old."

A few years and several hundred goals later, the kid came back to his first coach. At nine, he joined Titanic's Markham Waxer Atom AAA team. They would spend the next six years together, winning championships and creating a local legend.

"The game that sticks in my mind the most was in bantam at the Silver Stick Tournament in Port Huron. We were down 5-1 in the third, and he had the only goal. We called time-out with seven minutes left. He proceeded to set up a goal and score three more to tie it. Then he scored in overtime to win it."

I had heard enough of those yarns to finally go watch the kid play two winters ago. He left the rink with five points, and a dozen ridiculous YouTube-worthy moves. I left the rink knowing I'd never forget the name again.

Steven Stamkos.

I'm guessing you won't forget it either.

Stamkos will almost certainly be the first player taken in next June's NHL Draft. The vast majority of scouts and OHL coaches you talk to say they would take him before Tavares (who isn't eligible until 2009). He assisted on all three goals in the first game of the biggest junior tournament in the world against players two years older than him.

You might accuse me of local bias. You might be right.

It's hard not to cheerlead a little when the kid comes to your boy's hockey school just to help out. It's tough when his sister dances at the same school your daughter does. It's tough when everyone, *everyone*, who knows him, tells you what a wonderful young man he is.

"He's a phenomenal talent and a better person," says Alan Millar, GM of the Sarnia Sting, where Stamkos plays in the OHL. "He does things we've never seen before. Every day is a revelation."

I've talked to Steven only once, on a plane back from the NHL Draft last year (his agent had flown him and a few others down to get an idea what the experience will be like). He was just a regular teenager on a pretty cool end-of-school-year trip. You would never know he's a guy who does things with a puck that scouts with 40 years of experience say they've never seen before.

I know this isn't a new story. No fresh angle here. You've heard it all before. And you'll probably hear it again about another player next year. That's OK.

The World Juniors should be a time to puff your chest out about the kind of hockey players and young men this country is producing.

Especially when they live just down the street.

• • •

Postscript: *Stamkos was the first overall pick in the 2008 NHL Entry Draft. We aren't neighbours anymore. I moved to a little further north, to Aurora, Ontario. Steven moved to Tampa Bay. And NHL stardom. He scored 51 goals in 2009–10, sharing The Rocket Richard Trophy with Sidney Crosby.*

THE POLITICS OF PUCK

November 2008

Who says politics and hockey don't mix? A close examination of the US presidential race shows the two have never been more inter-twined.

In fact, the hockey-related opinions and puck policies of the can-didates may well decide the next leader of the free world. You think I'm kidding? Just take a look at the following actual quotes from the key figures in the race. (Now, I can't 100 per cent confirm the context of the statements, but I'm pretty sure I know what they were talking about.)

"I have fought against excessive spending my entire career, but we need to make it a priority to take care of our veterans."—Republican presiden-tial candidate John McCain, on the Daniel Alfredsson contract exten-sion.

"It's not something that I'm proud of. It was a mistake as a young man."—Democratic presidential candidate Barack Obama, on the time he bet on the Leafs to win the Cup.

"We have no choice but to eliminate the threat. This is a guy who is an extreme danger to the world."—Democratic vice-presidential candidate Joe Biden, on Sean Avery.

"May I call you Joe?"—Republican vice-presidential candidate Sarah Palin, upon meeting seldom-used Carolina Hurricane defenseman Josef Melichar.

"We've got a lot of pent-up anger and bitterness and misunderstanding. But the anger is real; it is powerful; and to simply wish it away, to condemn it without understanding its roots, only serves to widen the chasm of misunderstanding that exists."—Obama, addressing the Montreal Canadiens' feelings towards prospect Pavel Valentenko, who bolted for Russia.

"We're no longer staring into the abyss of defeat and we can now look ahead to the genuine prospect of success."—McCain, on the Phoenix Coyotes. Or maybe it was the Blackhawks. He gets confused sometimes.

"It's a crisis. It's a toxic mess, really,"—Palin, on the Atlanta Thrashers defence.

"I think he is a transformational figure... he has energized a lot of people around the world."—Former secretary of state Colin Powell, on Calgary Flames mascot Harvey the Hound.

"I think you may have noticed that Senator Obama's supporters have been saying some pretty nasty things about western Pennsylvania lately. And you know, I couldn't agree with them more!"—Though widely misinterpreted as a gaffe, McCain was actually revealing the disdain he shares, with Obama supporters, for the Penguins.

"Why can't I just eat my waffle?"—Obama, after being offered free Islanders tickets.

"All of 'em, any of 'em that have been in front of me over all these years."—Palin, when asked to name her favourite hockey player.

"I called him and asked him if he found anything offensive. And he just laughed and he said, 'Of course I don't. We all know what's going on.'"—Former president Bill Clinton, on his profanity-laced exchange with commissioner Gary Bettman, after they ran into each other at a Burger King in New York (Clinton was angry about unpenalized headshots).

"What Washington needs is adult supervision."—Obama, after watching Alexander Ovechkin and his teammates pretend to be a rock band for a team video.

"We are paying a very heavy price for the mismanagement—that's the kindest word I can give you."—McCain, a Leafs fan, commenting on the last 40-odd years of the franchise.

"The German asparagus are fabulous."—President George W. Bush. I actually don't have a hockey reference here. That's just my favourite George Bush quote I found on Google.

"You can put lipstick on a pig. It's still a pig."—Obama, commenting on the fact the *NHL on TSN* panel now wears more makeup because of High Definition.

• • •

Postscript: That last one was hurtful, but I was still glad he won.

THE HABS' SEASON OF CEREMONY

October 2008

This is not going to be a good season to be a Hab-hater. In fact, that's an understatement on the same scale as: "This is not a good month to be a stockbroker."

You either love or hate the Montreal Canadiens. There is no Middle Earth. If you love them, you are likely to have a winter of sheer bliss. If you despise them, if you gag at the mere mention of Les Glorieux, you are about to enter hockey's version of a Turkish prison. First of all, they look good. Really good. Second, and much more annoying to you, the next six months will seem like one interminable ceremony celebrating everything Bleu, Blanc et Rouge.

The Canadiens have hugantic plans for their 100th season. It all kicked off last Wednesday with the unveiling of the Ring of Honor, a wonderful tribute to the 44 former players and 10 builders in the Hockey Hall of Fame. Nobody does ceremonies as well as Montreal.

Or as often.

Welcome to Habapalooza. The schedule isn't even complete yet, and already we know the Ring of Honor ceremony will be followed by (brace yourself): Builder's Night (Oct. 28), Memorable Games in Canadiens History DVD release (Nov. 4), Patrick Roy's sweater retirement (Nov. 22), Opening of Centennial Plaza (Dec. 4), Centennial Gala (Dec. 5), NHL All-Star Weekend (Jan. 24–25), launch of the Canadiens Hall of Fame (April), NHL Draft (June 27), 8 "Vintage Jersey" games and two "Original Six Salute" games. Oh yeah, and the Stanley Cup Final* (June) (*tentative).

By contrast, the Nashville Predators event schedule consists of a 2-for-1 pizza night in February. That's it. (I'm kidding, of course. The Predators could never afford to give away free pizza slices.)

And I didn't even get to the Special Edition Montreal Canadiens Monopoly game, the commemorative stamps and a special-minted Habs Loonie (the only Canadian dollar that may rise in value this year).

The Canadiens, to their credit, want to give every fan at every game something special to remember about the centennial. But man, it's a long season. So filling out an entire home schedule worth of ceremonies is a challenge. Through my extensive sources within the organization (a mailroom intern named Miguel), I've uncovered some of the yet-to-be announced special celebrations on the Habs sked:

OCT. 25 (vs. Anaheim)–Book release party for the autobiography of Youppi, the Canadiens mascot, entitled: *Youppi: I really only like baseball, but I needed the money.*

NOV. 15 (vs. Philadelphia)–Chez Parée Appreciation Night, a touching ceremony in honor of the distraction (and subsequent losses) this legendary men's club has caused visiting teams for decades. A bronze statue of "Denise," Parée's longest serving stripper, will be unveiled outside the Bell Centre's North Entrance. (You will be able to sit near the statue, but you cannot make any physical contact.)

DEC. 21 (vs. Carolina)–Sergei Samsonov Sweater Retirement. After realizing they have already honored almost every living former player, the Habs are forced to commemorate the nine-goal, healthy scratch-filled 2006–07 season of this current Hurricane.

DEC. 25–The Canadiens attempt to rename Christmas "Habs Rule Day," so that the team can be properly feted each and every year by all of humanity. Jewish holiday also to be renamed "Habukkah."

JAN. 8 (vs. Toronto)–Leafs Mathematically Eliminated From Playoff Race Night*. Featuring post-game fireworks and dance party! Live Performance by Mitsou! (Mitsou is still a star in Quebec, 20 years later. I wonder if she kept all my letters?) (*May be cancelled if Leafs are already mathematically eliminated by January.)

FEB. 21 (vs. Ottawa)–Vito "The Plumber" Sweater Retirement. After officially running out of former players to honor with the Sergei Samsonov Sweater Retirement, the Habs hold a ceremony for the guy who fixed the clog in the men's bathroom in Section 201 during a key playoff game in 1993.

FEB. 24 (vs. Vancouver)–McDonald's begins giving out Limited Edition "Guys Georges Laraque Has Pummelled" figurines with Happy Meals. Riley Cote, Brian McGrattan, Brad May—they're all there! The "Bloodied Derek Boogaard" proves to be a favourite with the kids.

MARCH. 17 (vs. Rangers)–Rocket Richard Riot Recreation Night. To celebrate the 54th anniversary of the Riot, the first 10,000 fans in the building receive souvenir Molotov cocktails. City Chamber of Commerce co-operates to allow limited post-game looting.

APRIL. 11 (vs. Pittsburgh, last home game)–Ceremony honoring the best ceremonies of the season. Roy, Samsonov, Youppi, Vito, Denise… all in attendance. Not a dry eye in the house.

• • •

Postscript: *For some unknown reason, the aforementioned ceremonies never materialized. Such a shame. The countless other ceremonies the Canadiens did hold were all wonderful. But the season wasn't. After a fast start, the Habs floundered, and barely made the playoffs. They were quickly eliminated, in four straight losses to Boston. Dedicated Montreal fans were quick to look on the bright side: "Oh well, we'll get 'em next centennial!"*

PREMATURE EVALUATION:

AN EMBARRASSING MALE
(AND FEMALE) PROBLEM

October 2009

One week into the NHL season, and we residents of Hockeynation are already pretty sure of a few things:

- Colorado and Phoenix are unstoppable and will surely meet in the Western Conference Final.

- San Jose and Detroit suck, are likely headed for the draft lottery and are frantically sending their scouts to Windsor to watch Taylor Hall.

- Martin Brodeur and Roberto Luongo are stiffs, and if Team Canada selects them, they will lose 9-3 to Switzerland.

- The much-hyped Leafs defence couldn't stop that skating chimp from the MVP movies. Even if he was tranquilized.

- Alexander Ovechkin is going to score 90 goals, and 150 points. By Christmas.

OK, slight embellishments, perhaps. (Though after watching the first three Washington games, the last one might have a shot!)

But chances are, you've already heard similar bold declarations in some form of media, or from your buddies at work, or at the local tavern, coffee shop... bathhouse.

San Jose starts 0-2, and players are being asked, "Is it time to panic yet?" Luongo gives up a couple of softies and they boo him and beg for Andrew Raycroft. I read somewhere online the other day that Ray Emery is the "early favourite for Comeback Player-of-the-Year." He'd played TWO GAMES!

Yes, we sports fans suffer from the embarrassing medical condition known as Premature Evaluation (PE).

PE is hardly a new problem. Rushing to judgment is human nature. We hope (Flames fans) or fear (Leaf fans) that what we've seen in one week might just be the reality of the next six months. If you haven't seen your team play a good game yet, maybe they... never will. And what excited poolie hasn't projected statistics from three games into a full season—Mike Richards: 135 goals, 0 assists!

But PE has now reached full pandemic status. We live in a bubble of endless blogs, tweets, "long-time listener, first-time caller" radio shows and TV hockey panels that crave instant and definitive analysis. (Yes, there is a heavy dose of *mea culpa*, or at least *wea culpa*, in this rant.) We want judgments handed down NOW, even if we've only seen a tiny fragment of the evidence.

I've dubbed it Premature Evaluation in hopes the *American Journal of Medicine* will publish this paper, and give me the credibility in the scientific community I've long deserved. But the truth is, for years my buddies and I had another name for PE: "Drafting a Larry."

When I was 16, I organized my first baseball fantasy league (it was still just called a "pool" back then). We did our draft after the season had started, on the day Larry Herndon of the Detroit Tigers hit home runs in four straight at-bats. In what was clearly a sign of the early stages of PE, I figured this meant Herndon was good for about 80 HRs on the year.

So I picked him first overall.

Larry hit 23 home runs. Not bad, but about half as many as a dozen other guys I should have taken before him. In a dark, sadistic twist, my sister won the pool, with Mike Schmidt, Andre Dawson and Gorman Thomas on her team. Larry Herndon still haunts me to this day.

Ever since, when one of us made a ridiculous statement early in a season, like "The Bengals are 2-1, they're going to the playoffs!" he would immediately be called out:

"Dude, you just drafted a Larry!"

Safe to say we've all drafted a few Larrys in our time.

And yet, we all know what's going to happen. As the season rolls along, reality, and the law of averages, takes over. The hot streaks cool down. The cool streaks heat up. Luongo and Brodeur will be great again. François Beauchemin will not be minus 47. The Avalanche will fall back in the pack and Sharks will climb back near the top (only to lose in round one).

So let's save ourselves from ourselves. From now on, let's impose a ban on all discussion and evaluation of anything that happens in the first... say... five games of the season. A simple two-week blackout on any dumb PE of NHL teams and players.

No overdramatic newspaper headlines when a team is 0-1-1. No panic-mongering on hockey chat-sites when your goalie gets yanked in his third start. No TV panels asking if some free agent signing "looks like a bust" after he gets one assist in his first four games. (We'll just bring back the monkey to fill our intermissions—let her spin the wheel... maybe ride a unicycle... or do what she usually did: fling her poo at me.)

Five measly games. Is it really asking too much? One brief holiday from hysteria?

Personally, I would have pushed for 10 games, but before the season, I asked an NHL star if he thought his team was any good. He texted back, "Gimme the first five games and I'll tell you."

Fine. Five games it is then. A collective stint in PE Rehab. After that, we can all start firing coaches, trading overpaid stars that aren't producing, declaring guys Comeback Player-of-the-Year candidates...

... and buying Coyotes playoff tickets. (Make the cheque out to Judge Baum.)

• • •

Postscript: *The Premature Evaluations of 2009 were, as per usual, mostly wrong. San Jose and Detroit did turn it around, as did Brodeur and Luongo. And Alexander Ovechkin fell 40 goals short of 90. But Colorado and Phoenix did surprise everyone and made the playoffs.*

MAGIC KARPET RIDES

January 2004

It was the kid on the Krazy Karpet who brought it all back.

I'd just jogged out of the woods when he took me out. Made me do a full Bobby Orr over him as he flew across the path and rammed the snow bank at the bottom of the hill.

"Sorry, man," he muttered as he got up and ran back past me without bothering a glance. *No time, man. Gotta get back up there.*

Can't blame him. When you've waited until mid-January for snow to cover the only decent vertical in your neighbourhood, there's no time to waste.

I stood and watched for a while. There were only three of them, two on Karpets, and one on that thing with the mini-skis and the steering wheel. Up and down they went. Side by side, into each other, over each other, oblivious to the fact the snow was already warming into a nasty rain and their hill was turning to slushy mud.

Damn, was I jealous.

Life has no better age than 10, no better time than the first snow, no better ride than a Krazy Karpet, and no better place than Your Hill.

We all had Our Hill. Mine was just a Kurt Warner bomb away from my front door. We were three houses from the end of a street that backed onto Ottawa's Greenbelt, a stretch of woods and ravines that went on forever (a kid's forever, anyway).

Our Hill was pure perfection. Maybe six storeys high, a three-point shot wide, trees lining either side, with an incline steep enough to scare you on an icy day, and send you halfway across the open field at the bottom on a hard-packed track.

My buddy Syl's backyard rink was lit, so it could wait until after dinner. After school, we lived on the hill.

It wasn't a sport. It was a bunch of them.

- Races down.

- Races back up.

- Individual time trials.

- Carefully judged freestyling off the jumps.

- Distance events (who would slide furthest out onto the field at the bottom—"And no pushing off the snow for a few extra feet at the end, ya cheater!").

- Full-contact suicide runs ("Last guy still on wins!").

It was the Ironman, on a cheap piece of purple plastic.

Has Mankind (the species, not the wrestler) ever come up with anything better than the Krazy Karpet? The way it would perpetually roll itself up into that easy-carrying cylinder, except for the ride down when it was as flat as you could lie, for as long as you could hold on.

On a Karpet, you felt every inch of the hill. Each little bump was a legitimate threat to future procreation. To this day, when I look at my son and daughter in wonder, I give thanks for the extra padding in my snow pants.

Of course, there were advantages. By Grade 7 or so, when the occasional girl would tag along, we'd go doubles on the Karpet. If you sat at the back, and hit a bump just right, you made second base instantly.

I've always loved the Karpet better than those big metal battle-ship toboggans. Likely because once, under a sea of snowsuits and humanity, my face somehow got lodged under the front end, where it remained for the duration of the run over hard crusty snow (insert your mandatory "That explains a lot" thought here).

When we all got up at the bottom, my friends gave me the pat-ented "Jennifer Love Hewitt When She Sees the Psycho Killer with the Giant Fishhook Behind Her in the Mirror" look.

Seems I was a dead ringer for Leatherface. My mug had been slashed all over in these bizarre inch-long lines, reminiscent of Gerry Cheevers's old goalie mask. The following month is still referred to as my awkward mutant phase.

One year, Dad bought me a pair of old wooden cross-country skis at the annual Winter Exchange. Since I felt cross-country skiing was only for Norwegians and sadists, particularly Norwegian sadists, we mostly used them on the hill.

We'd build a jump two-thirds down, and then take off from the top, make-believing we were Horst Bulau (I'm guessing there aren't many kids today pretending they're Horst Bulau). We'd get about a second of hang time, and then thrust both arms in the air when we nailed the landing.

We won more Olympic medals on that hill than the Cuban box-ing team.

Of course, more often than not, we landed like the "Agony of Defeat" guy on the opening of Wide World of Sports.

I once knocked myself out after we built the ramp too steep. The skis just stopped, catapulting me skyward like the Monty Python cow. I now believe it was a grade 3 concussion. And I was in Grade 4. Figures. I was always behind a grade.

These were the winters of my content.

Up and down my hill. Sliding, screaming, scrapping, leaping, tumbling, laughing. And finally, when it got too dark to see the bot-tom, and dinner was ready an hour ago, and one mitt was lost some-where under the snow...

We'd do 10 more runs.

Then we'd head home, trying to step in the same Cougar boot-prints we'd made on the way there, our faces and toes so numb we couldn't feel anything.

Except pure bliss.

• • •

Postscript: *A couple of years back, we were looking at houses in the town we were planning on moving to. On one street, the real estate agent says, "Your kids might like this. Just behind the trees over there is the biggest toboggan hill in town." Sold. I'm not saying it was the reason we bought there. But it clinched the deal.*

THE MONKEY PROPHECIES

May 2003

Before we start, let's make one thing clear. I didn't want to write about the monkey.

The monkey is my nemesis. I now spend several hours a day answering emails about the monkey. Colleagues address me as "Monkey-Boy." My three-year-old son told his nursery school class that his Dad works at a zoo (actually, that's pretty much accurate). Beautiful women stop me in the street, only to ask me what the monkey is like.

You want to know what the monkey is like? The first time I met her, she peed on my shoe. The dry cleaner is having trouble getting the monkey-smell out of my suits. And in all likelihood, the monkey will be hosting the show next year, and I will be doing The Seniors' Shuffleboard Tournament on community cable.

Insecure, fragile, jealous TV ego-heads like myself can't handle this kind of threat. I now have poaching dreams.

If you don't know Maggie the Monkey, she is, with apologies to the wonderful Jennifer Hedger, the hottest thing on the network.

She was brought in just before the start of the playoffs in the name of science… and cheap ratings ploys.

We wanted to prove once and for all that so-called "expert" predictions are a farce in the always-unpredictable Stanley Cup Playoffs. So in comes Maggie, a crab-eating macaque from the Bowmanville Zoo east of Toronto. (By the way, if you're ever bored, just say "macaque" over and over with a Boston accent… it's endless hours of fun.)

Anyway, the monkey spins a wheel and picks the Ducks to upset the Wings, and we all say "How cute!" And then the Ducks win, and she picks them again over the Stars, and the Ducks win again, and she picks them again over the Wild, and the Ducks keep winning, and suddenly the Prophet Monkey is a cult hero.

And thus, I've been reduced to the position of monkey-publicist, taking calls from reporters as far away as California, and being deluged with questions from you like:

"What's the monkey's record?"

"Does the monkey handicap the NBA, too?

"Is the monkey single?"

Cute. Real cute. But since you won't leave me alone, I am here to answer your monkey questions. Actually, I had a better idea. With the help of groundbreaking monkey sign language developed by Matthew Broderick and his team of scientists in *Project X*, I interviewed the monkey myself.

JD: "Tell me about your background."

MM: (angrily) "Please end your questions with 'O Great One,' as my agent stipulated when I agreed to this."

JD: "Fine. Tell me about your background, O Great One."

MM: "That's better. Well, I lived in the jungle until I was captured by a man with a big yellow hat." (laughs) "My *Curious George* material is pure gold."

JD: "Okaaay. How do you explain your stunning success in predicting those Anaheim upsets?"

MM: (waits)

JD: "O Great One."

MM: "Hockey is in my blood. I was up for the lead in that MVP movie about the hockey-playing monkey. It was bull$*#@ I didn't get it. That chimp slept with somebody."

JD: "That's sick."

MM: "It's a dirty business, pal."

JD: "But really, why the Ducks, O Great One? Had you been charting Giguere's consistent statistical improvement over the last three years? Did you, like Kariya, buy into the defence-first mentality? Or is it the fact their PIMs per game is a paltry 7.8?"

MM: "Actually, there's a duck that sneaks me cigarettes at the zoo. So I figured I owed the species."

JD: "Is there any connection between you and the Rally Monkey that led the Anaheim Angels to the World Series title?"

MM: "Don't compare me to some stuffed toy people wave around at a game. I'm a God."

JD: "Do you have a mentor, or anyone you look up to?"

MM: "Marcel, Ross's monkey from *Friends*. He really broke down the barriers for macaques. Before Marcel, it was all about chimps and orangutans. Marcel opened a lot of doors in the business."

JD: "What's next for you?"

MM: "You name it. Endorsements. Psychic hotlines. Movies. I'm talking with Sigourney Weaver about remaking *Gorillas in the Mist*."

JD: "But... you're... not a... gorilla."

MM: "I've spoken to De Niro about how he put on the weight for the end of *Raging Bull*. Gorilla is not that tough. I can do gorilla."

JD: "Will the Ducks win it all?"

MM: "Sorry, kid. You'll have to wait like anyone else. We're in negotiations with the networks for a prime-time "Monkey-Prophet Picks the Cup Winner" special. We might do it live from Times Square. Dick Clark's involved."

JD: "But... TSN discovered you!"

MM: "C'mon, kid, be realistic. You're Canadian cable. The Monkey Prophet has outgrown you. I'll talk to my people. We'll get you a goat or something."

JD: "Gee, thanks."

MM: (waits)
JD: "... O Great One."

• • •

Postscript: *I really did hate that monkey. That is, until one year when they decided to liven things up by bringing in a lemur. We called it "Jacques Lemur," another fine example of our highbrow comedy. The lemur sat on my head and dug its claws into my skull. We were live on TV, so I had to smile and keep talking, but I could feel this slow trickle of blood running down the back of my neck. I got the lemur fired. And gained a new appreciation for the monkey. Maggie the Macaque retired from NHL on TSN after the 2009 Stanley Cup Playoffs. She was getting old, and could barely spin the wheel. She never recaptured the magic of her 2003 Anaheim prophecies, finishing with a career prediction record well under .500. Typical, isn't it? She has a great rookie season, signs the big contract and then under-performs the rest of her career.*

DUCHENE AND HODGSON:

BOYHOOD PALS NOW A WORLD APART

October 2009

You'd be hard pressed to find two better young men than Matt Duchene and Cody Hodgson. They are like genetic lab-creations of what Canada wants its hockey players to be: ridiculously talented, passionate, hard-working, team-first guys. And for the Hockey Moms out there, they are also polite, modest, well spoken and I can pretty much guarantee they'll have your daughter home on time.

You'd also be hard pressed to find two hockey lives so intertwined. Two careers, twinned since tyke.

Until now, that is.

Over the last month, their parallel paths took hard turns in different directions. One is skating on clouds, playing big minutes on the NHL's surprise team. The other is at home, off skates until a doctor says otherwise, thinking next year can't come soon enough.

First, the back-story.

Duchene and Hodgson both grew up in the small town of Haliburton, Ontario. There was only one tyke rep team there, so both were on it—six-year-old Cody at centre, five-year-old Matt on his wing. The weak-ankled beginnings of a lifelong friendship, built on a shared dream.

"We talked about it all the time playing mini sticks as kids—going to the NHL some day," says Hodgson. "But I guess you never really believe it would happen to both of us."

Hodgson would move south to Markham after those tyke years, but the two would play against each other all winter, then team up again in the summer on a travelling team coached by Duchene's father. The team was called "Kids Love Hockey," after the sponsor. Appropriate name.

"Those were great times," Hodgson says. "We had a ton of fun."

"We won just about everything," adds Duchene. "It was awesome."

Hodgson was drafted by the OHL's Brampton Battalion in 2006. Sure enough, Brampton also called Duchene's name one year later.

Through junior, they were teammates in the winter, and training partners in the summer—two kids/one obsession/365 days a year.

"At our cottage near Haliburton, I'd ride my bike down in the summer, work out, and then shoot pucks at Matt's place," says Hodgson. "He had a great set-up... a goalie he built in shop class that has all the same holes a goalie in the butterfly has. It was amazing."

Duchene even had special headgear—mosquito nets to fight off those pesky cottage-country predators.

Those endless summer days fighting bugs and firing pucks paid off, big time. Hodgson was drafted 10th overall by Vancouver in 2008. Duchene went third overall to Colorado one June later.

The perfect ending would have been for both to make their NHL teams this season—live the dream together. It was Hodgson, most believed, who had the best shot to stick. He already had one pro camp under his belt, and had been sensational at the World Juniors. Duchene was still just a pup at 18.

But that's when things went askew.

Hodgson hurt his back training in the summer. At camp, he was diagnosed with a herniated disc, but cleared to play. Yet, he never felt right. All the power seemed to have bled from his legs.

The Canucks sent him back to Brampton. He was crushed.

A second opinion from the Cleveland Clinic confirmed the herniated disc. But doctors there recommended he stay off skates indefinitely.

Then it got worse. Canucks coach Alain Vigneault inferred Hodgson was using the injury as an excuse for a poor camp, trying to "roll the [blame] in a different direction." It was an odd thing to say about your franchise's number one prospect. Some twisted motivational technique, perhaps.

The words stung the kid. But he refuses to fire back—saying something negative about the organization that drafted him is not in Hodgson's DNA.

"The Canucks medical staff has been very supportive of everything I've done," he says. Besides that, he'd rather not talk about it.

Meanwhile, it was a fall fantasy for Matt Duchene. Joe Sakic had retired, and the Avs were rebuilding. There were jobs to be had. He had a great camp, made the team and quickly left little doubt he would be staying beyond every junior player's magic number of 10 games.

"I'm just ecstatic about everything," Duchene says. "I'm living the dream. I remember my second pre-season game against St. Louis, I was taking the faceoff against Keith Tkachuk, and Paul Kariya was on his wing. I have a picture of me with Paul Kariya when I was eight years old at Maple Leaf Gardens. I treasured that growing up. Now I look over and he's on the wing against me. Unreal."

And as if he needed more to be pumped about, his team leads the Western Conference.

So here we are. The boyhood pals from Haliburton—whose careers had matched each other stride for stride—are suddenly in very different places. Literally and emotionally.

"I know it's been really tough on Cody," says Duchene. "I gave him his space for a while when he was sent back. But he texted me after we beat Vancouver, and after I scored my first goal, just to say congrats. He's such a character guy, he'll be fine."

Hodgson is getting a little closer to "fine" every day. His back is finally starting to feel right again. He hopes to be cleared to skate next week. And the fact his old tyke winger is "living the dream" without him is anything but a downer.

"I'm thrilled to see Matt doing so well. In fact, watching him and JT (John Tavares) and Del Zotto all have success, it energizes me. Because I played with those guys, so when they do well up there, I know I can, too."

• • •

Postscript: *Hodgson missed most of the season with his back injury, but did return to Brampton for the playoffs. Duchene, meanwhile, put together a brilliant NHL rookie season, scoring 25 goals, and getting nominated for the Calder Trophy. The two remain good friends.*

THE GIFT OF GIRLS

September 2009

When my wife and I were starting a family, my Mom would always say, "It doesn't matter if you have boys or girls, as long as they have the right number of fingers and toes."

Under my breath, I would add: "… and powerful thighs and soft hands that will someday be worthy of a full Ivy League hockey scholarship." (Football, soccer, and track would do, too. I'm not fussy when it comes to free tuition at prestigious schools.)

Look, I'm a sports guy. So yes, I wanted sports kids. It was shallow, narrow, and selfish, but… honest.

I always figured all my children would be boys. There was no logical rationale for this belief. In fact, I probably should have guessed the opposite. I have two sisters, my father had three, and my mother, one. My wife's side looks even more like *The View*. She is one of three girls, her Mom is one of four.

And even if genes are irrelevant, the last time I checked, gender odds were about the same as a pre-game coin-flip. Boy or girl, kick or receive. Only difference is, with the former, you can't defer.

In retrospect, my boy-only belief stemmed purely from fear. All I knew was boy stuff. Flowered dresses, ballet slippers, the ability to do proper pigtails—these things terrified me.

Sure, I knew that girls could bend it like Beckham, and go backhand shelf, too. But they are intricate, complicated, creatures. Boys are simple. Run. Eat. Pee. Sleep. Repeat. They just seemed easier.

It's not that I didn't want a little girl. We thought one of each would be perfect, like that pretend family of models you see in the travel magazines. (I believe my wife wanted one of each, *and* the male model from the travel magazines, but I digress.)

I just figured the higher powers that decide these things wouldn't trust a poorly-rounded, sport-obsessed, caveman like me to raise a girl properly. So they'd just make everyone's life easier, and toss us two boys.

So when the doctors pulled out our first child, I believe I yelled, to no one in particular, "Penis! Told ya!"

I actually had a blue Nerf mini-football with me at the hospital. Like the boy was going have his umbilical cord cut, get cleaned up, and immediately want to run a down-out-down for me. I was taking dumb-ass to a whole new level.

But my guess had been right. A boy it was, and thus boys it would surely be.

Except 18 months later, back in the hospital for the arrival of winger number two, something odd happened. There was no penis.

That's weird, I thought. I'd never seen a guy without one. (And this was years before Lady Gaga.)

I had a baby daughter.

And two years later, we got a little crazy, and out popped another one.

Final score in our house: 3-2 Girls. A shocker. I think I heard Al Michaels in the delivery room screaming, "Do you believe in miracles?!? Yes!!!"

Suddenly, my whole world turned pink. I was sucked into a vortex of My Little Pony, Dora, American Girl dolls, and endless dance classes and recitals. It was foreign, it was frightening, it was...

... heaven.

Daughters turn men to mush. Instant oatmeal. Sure, we pretend we're Mel Gibson in *Braveheart* in our Sunday beer leagues. Then we start bawling the first time they bring us a hand-drawn card with a heart on it.

My two little girls are the most gorgeous, precious living entities in the history of the universe. Yes, I know. Every bragging father makes that claim. But I'm the one that's right.

Darian, the oldest, is a blond and beautiful, sings like an angel, and makes friends faster than Facebook. Her little sister Gracie is a feisty brunette with Bette Davis eyes and a sense of humor worthy of her own sitcom.

I fell so madly in love with them that the whole "I want sports kids" thing didn't matter anymore. OK, maybe it still mattered a bit.

Neither showed much interest in playing sports early on. Their brother Jared plays rep hockey, so they got dragged to the rink four times a week, and weren't too interested in going back to skate themselves.

So we turned to soccer.

Watching them play was a major adjustment for me. When my boy gets hurt, I just dust him off and send him back out there, as my Dad did to me. Like John Mayer sings, "Boys you can break, you find out how much they can take." (Please don't tell my friends I quoted a John Mayer song.)

But my girls, I just wanted to protect. One little raspberry on their knee and I wanted to wrap them in blankets and feed them ice cream. If they got kicked in the shin by somebody's little Emma or Victoria, I waited in the parking lot for that kid and took her Freezie. (Not really, but I thought about it.)

And there were other challenges. Darian's first season (she was five), she ran harder than anyone, up and down the field. One minor problem: she refused to go anywhere near the ball.

"Go get it!" I'd yell. The look I'd get back was a distinct, "Why?" That stupid round thing was just getting in the way of her wind sprints.

Soon she grew tired of the running and began to negotiate her playing time down.

This is an actual exchange (I typed it my blackberry as soon as it happened, thinking I would read it to her someday after she won back-to-back NCAA soccer titles):

Coach: "Darian, I need you back out there, just for five minutes!"

Darian: "How about one minute?"

Coach (bewildered and desperate): "Umm… three minutes?"

Darian (slowly getting up off the grass): "I'll go for two. Dad, time it."

No, I didn't weep. (Until later, when I was alone.)

But she kept playing, and now loves it, putting on her uniform five hours before the game, and begging *not* to come off. *"Please coach, five more minutes!"*

During Game Seven of the 2009 Stanley Cup final in Detroit, I got a call from her: "Dad, I scored my first goal tonight!" I immediately resented the Red Wings for losing Game 6, and making me miss that moment. I sulked for the rest of the night, and was quietly pleased when the Penguins won. *"See what you get for messing with my family, Osgoode?"*

Gracie, my littlest, was a different animal (emphasis on the animal part). Last year was her first in soccer. She was a foot shorter and 10 pounds lighter than any other girl on the field. But if you took the ball off her, you were going down.

One evening, as we drove home from a game, she sipped from her juice-box, and said, matter-of-factly, "Dad, I made three girls cry tonight."

"Yes, you did honey. Yes you did."

I think I teared up again. I've rarely been prouder.

• • •

Postscript: Darian is 8, now. Gracie is 6. Besides dance, they are in soccer, yoga, skating, swimming. I actually said to my wife the other day, "We really have got to cut down on these sports." I'm still trying to figure out if that's progress or sacrilege.

WHAT THEY REALLY MEAN

October 2002

We are being Nuked. In the papers, at the podiums, in the post-game scrums, poor helpless sports fans are being bombarded by Nukes.

Brief pause for definition: Nuke—a noun derived from the character Nuke Laloosh, Tim Robbins' strong-armed, dim-witted pitcher in the movie *Bull Durham*.

Crash Davis (played by legendary Sioux Indian actor "Dances with Wolves") taught Nuke all the lame clichés he'd need to make it through interviews in The Show. Today, they call that "Media Training." Athletes are being taught how to avoid answering questions before they're even drafted, which turns their entire careers into one long series of repetitious, often fictitious, clichés. Nukes are everywhere, and there's no shelter for the helpless fan.

Cue the loud infomercial announcer: "That's why you need the new NUKE-ENGLISH DICTIONARY! A complete translation guide for jocktalk! Keep it by your side when watching *SportsCenter* or reading the morning paper! You'll finally understand what your heroes are really saying! Just $19.95 (plus postage and handling)! Here's a sample!"

PRE-GAME:
"We can't take this team too lightly."

(TRANSLATION: "They're 2-34. Our mascot might get a triple-double!")

"We're peaking at the right time."

("Most of the guys are right at the end of a steroid cycle.")

"I play every game like it's my last."

("It's my last game. I'm about to be indicted on a felony.")

"There's no I in Team."

("But there's one in 'Incentive Clause,' so I ain't passing to anybody.")

"I don't read the papers."

("I don't know how to read.")

POST-GAME:
"It was a total team effort."

("It was basically all me.")

"We just didn't have it tonight."

("We were out clubbing 'til 6 a.m., and man were we hung over.")

"I love coaching this team. These guys played their hearts out for me, and they have nothing to be ashamed of. We'll get 'em next year!"

("I'm soooo fired.")

FREE-AGENCY:
"It's not about the money."

("Did you see all those zeros?! Woo-Hoo! I'm Bill Gates, baby!")

"I wanted to play here because this is a beautiful city and a great (INSERT SPORT HERE) town."

("Did you see all those zeros?! Woo-Hoo!")

"It's about taking care of my family."

("I have 12 different kids from nine different mothers, and two more paternity suits pending, so I really need the money.")

LEGAL TROUBLE:
"I didn't do it."

("I paid someone else to do it.")

"It was just a misunderstanding."

("Someone misunderstood me, so I slugged 'em.")

"That bag of drugs you found in my car isn't mine... Ah, it's my cousin Lenny's."

("Oh crap. I don't even have a cousin named Lenny.")

RETIREMENT:
"I want to spend more time with my family."

("I want to play 36 holes a day, and get my handicap under 5.")

"You're the best fans in the world! Thanks for your support!"

("You're the best groupies in the world! Thanks for your discretion!")

"I'm leaving under my own terms."

("My agent called everybody and even the Thrashers won't sign my washed-up sorry ass.")

• • •

Postscript: *I just watched* Bull Durham *the other day on TBS. It holds up amazingly well after all these years. So does my Nuke-English Dictionary, now available online in 27 different jock-cliché languages.*

OTTAWA'S FATAL FLAW

April 2008

In the wake of Ottawa's early exit from the playoffs, just about every-body has been blamed. They blamed the coach/GM. They blamed the forwards. They blamed the guy who installed that mural, outside Pittsburgh's locker room, of the Senators beating the Penguins last year (never a good idea to give Sid extra motivation). They blamed the lame actor who portrayed a gladiator in the pre-game (I've seen better acting in my *Best of Dolph Lundgren* DVD). And of course, they blamed the goalie.

No, Martin Gerber didn't cost the Senators the series against Pittsburgh. Not even close. Ray Emery didn't cost them the final last year against Anaheim, either. Goaltenders have never been the only reason Ottawa has lost. But here's the rub: they've never been the only reason Ottawa has won, either.

Oh sure, there's some regular season games you could dig up where one of them stood on his head, but almost every NHL goalie gets freakishly hot on occasion. Brian Boucher once had five shutouts in a row. Nuff said.

To make a team truly great, you need a goalie who will single-handedly steal you a game once-in-a-while in the playoffs. Someone to inspire, instead of deflate. Someone to make that ridiculous somersaulting, momentum-turning, spill-your-beer-on-your-lap, series-saving stop. (Then not let in a softie three minutes later.)

Emery and Gerber are what every Senators goalie in the modern history of this franchise has been: average, decent, pedestrian. And if you are a fan of this team, those are swear words, every one.

Say what you want about trade deadline failures, defensive lapses and Heatley and Spezza's face-on-the-milk carton performances. The tragic flaw of this franchise is, and always has been, the absence of a Cup-calibre goalie.

If the window has closed on this "core," if this is somehow the end of a decade-long run of parade-possible teams who just couldn't finish, that would be the epitaph: *OTTAWA SENATORS 1997–2008. GOOD TEAM. NEEDED A GOALIE.*

The last tender I recall stealing games at clutch times was Ron Tugnutt, the first year they made the playoffs. And I had to think about it for a while. When the best money-goalie your memory can come up with is a journeyman who was roughly the size of Prince, you have issues.

Sure, Patrick Lalime was far better than the giggle-lines most writers and broadcasters use him for (I plead guilty). His career play-off goals-against (1.77) is still among the best in NHL history. But all those horrific goals at the worst of times have forever branded him as Ottawa's Bill Buckner.

The saddest short story ever written for Sens fans can be found on page 179 of the team media guide. It's the list labelled "All-Time Roster: Goaltenders/Gardiens de But" (or as my buddy Brad translates it: butt-gardeners). WARNING: if you're a weeper, grab a tissue. Or a towel.

It reads: Mike Bales, Tom Barrasso (10 years too late), Don Beaupre, Daniel Berthiaume, Craig Billington, Emery, Mike Fountain, Gerber, Dominik Hasek (wonky groin edition), Jani Hurme, Mark LaForest, Simon Lajeunesse, Lalime, Darrin Madeley, Mike Morrison,

Martin Prusek, Damian Rhodes, Peter Sidorkiewicz, Tugnutt, Steve Weeks.

Yowsa. For full effect, the reading of that list really should be accompanied by a bugler playing "Taps".

The Senators have long been praised for their solid drafting. But amidst all the good forward and defensive finds, not a single keeper who's been a... well... keeper. You'd think in 15 seasons, they might have stumbled onto one masked stud. Even by mistake. Nope.

And consider the ones who have slipped away. Let's play every Senator fan's (and scout's) least-favourite game show: WHO YOU COULDA HAD!

In 1994, your Ottawa Senators selected goalie Bryan Masotta 81st overall. OK, Bob, tell them "Who You Coulda Had!"

Deep-voiced Announcer Guy: "You coulda had... Marty Turco, 43 spots later! But wait, it gets better! Your Senators also chose Frederic Cassivi in the 9th round, just before Tim Thomas, Tomas Vokoun and Evgeni Nabokov!"

Ouch. All-righty, round two. In 1999, you selected the legendary Simon Lajeunesse in the second round, 48th overall. Bob?

"You coulda had... Ryan Miller... 90 picks later!"

And now the brainteasing bonus round. In 1998, you drafted Mathieu Chouinard. After failing to sign him, you drafted him again in 2000, 45th overall! Bob?

"Yes, James, for a guy you drafted twice and who never played a single game for you, you coulda had... 155 spots later... Henrik Lundquist! Sorry, you lose. Again! Next time on WHO YOU COULDA HAD, we revisit 1993, the year the Senators drafted can't-miss goalie-prospect, Toby Kvalevog! Goodnight, everybody!"

By the way, about that Mathieu Chouinard-Double-Doh! It's officially number two on the all-time Ottawa sports draft follies, just behind the Rough Riders drafting the dead guy.

Of course, it's not just the draft. There have been franchise goalies available through trades and free agency, but Ottawa has always struck out.

John Muckler kicked tires on Roberto Luongo just before he was dealt to the Canucks. Mike Keenan, then the Panthers GM, says they talked about a deal (Emery, Antoine Vermette, a defenceman and a draft pick was one possibility), but he could never get Muckler to get serious.

"I told John make me a firm offer," Keenan says. "But he never did." So Keenan traded Luongo to the Canucks.

So here we are. A full decade as a contender, and the Senators still search for that one goalie they can pencil in for the next six seasons. The guy who would make the D play with confidence and creativity, instead of sheer terror. The guy who would help the scorers relax because they know they don't need four or five to win every night.

I know. There is only a handful of those around. But the one black mark on this franchise remains its failure to find one.

• • •

Postscript: *At the time of writing, Ottawa's goaltending tandem is Pascal Leclaire and Brian Elliott. Both are solid, though neither looks like the savior Ottawa fans continue to wait for. Fifteen years, and counting.*

JUNGLE LOVE

September 2005

It seemed like a relatively innocent, dare I say romantic, inquiry.

My wife was approaching a landmark birthday (revealing the actual number would likely lead to beheading, or something worse, like say, having to watch *Gray's Anatomy* with her). So, in a weak moment a couple of months back, I offered the following:

"If I could give you anything in the world for your birthday, what would you want?"

She came up with several ideas, which were rejected due to infeasibility. No, honey, rounds of golf cannot be universally reduced to six holes. No, the NFL will not fold, leaving Sunday afternoons exclusively for fashion and home design shows. No, Expedia.ca does not offer "Sponge Bathing David Beckham" tours.

But after a couple of days of quiet pondering, she had her answer:

"I want us to go on a vegetarian yoga retreat in the jungle of Costa Rica."

Uh… *Que?*

The "vegetarian" and "yoga retreat" parts didn't really surprise me. That's just how she rolls. Even the "Costa Rica" idea barely twitched an eyebrow. I'll take a tropical beach any way. It was those other two words she kind of casually chucked in there: "JUNGLE" and "US."

Look, I do all-inclusive beach resorts with cute little umbrella drinks and hot salsa teachers named Juanita. I don't do jungle. I don't really do yoga either, though I occasionally stretch before beer league touch football games, if that counts for anything.

"Oooh, that sounds amazing, baby. But maybe you want to do this one with the girls… you know… chick-bonding… Ya-Ya Sisterhood… that kinda deal."

"No. I want to do this together."

Long silence.

"Now, by jungle, you mean a couple of palm trees, a coconut and maybe one of those cute little lizards on our balcony, right?"

"No. I mean jungle. As in a hut on a mountain in the middle of the rain forest."

Longer silence.

"TV?"

"No."

"Pool?"

"No."

"Gym?"

"No. But four hours of yoga a day. Beginning at 7:00 each morning. In the jungle."

Extremely long silence intended. But instead I believe a tiny terrified school-girlish shriek slipped out. It resembled the yelp of a chihuahua when you step on its paw.

"Umm. You know I saw these diamond earrings at Tiffany's."

"Too late. I already booked it."

Oh.

So here I am, two weeks before hockey season, cramped in the back of a minivan filled with eight vegetarian female yogis intently discussing their respective "energies" and "auras," bouncing along something that vaguely resembles a road, five hours from San Jose, Costa Rica, and climbing into nowhere.

Finally, just as I figure we can't possibly go any further, we switch to a hardcore four-wheeler that crawls the last couple of miles up the mountain to our "nature reserve"—a name, by the way, with which I wholeheartedly concur. RESERVED FOR NATURE. HUMANS STAY OUT!

Seriously. We are deeeeeep. I swear I see one of those Kalahari Bushmen running past me saying: "Dude, this is way too scary for me. I'm out." I'm figuring Jane Goodall is about to tiptoe out of the mist, whispering: "Shhhh. The gorillas are mating now. Crouch and observe. Crouch and observe."

Plus, it was night. Nothing like wandering through the jungle in pitch-black trying to find your hut while hearing 187 creepy sounds you've never heard before.

"Hmm. Honey... was that python swallowing rat, or jaguar crapping? Hard to tell really."

The huts were actually quite spacious. In fact, there was room for more than 300 species of insects. I felt like Agent freakin' Starling stumbling into Buffalo Bill's bug room in *Silence of the Lambs*.

Moths. Spiders. Beetles. Mosquitoes. Each one three times the size of North American bugs. Seriously. These suckers are on both The Clear and The Cream. This one coackroachy thing was roughly the size of my shoe, and had antennae longer than our roll of dental floss. It was a 1950s B–monster movie. Thankfully, it also made for an all-you-can-eat buffet for the two dozen or so geckos co-tenanting with us.

We spent most of the night with our tiny flashlight pointed at the wall, watching the lizards eat the bugs. Darn fine entertainment, actually. Should be a Fox show. I think I got a solid 40 minutes of sleep. Before the howler monkeys started screaming.

You know... that scream they scream before they abandon their boring fruit and berries diet, and decide to swarm and eat helpless tourists. Yeah, that scream.

Happy birthday, honey.

Any chance there's a Westin nearby?

• • •

Postscript: *See next column.*

JUNGLE LOVE, PART 2

September 2005

Hey! Any Hollywood director–types out there putting the final touches on a new horror flick? Well, I have found your soundtrack. There are few noises weirder and eerier than the 5 a.m. jungle wake-up call that is the scream of the howler monkey.

It is night one in a hut in the Costa Rican jungle. For hours, we have listened to a live performance of the hot new CD "Strange Animal Noises Just Outside Your Door Which You Can't and Don't Want To Identify!" (Club mix.) Then, just before dawn comes this ghostly wail. Apparently, howler monkeys fancy themselves as the jungle's wake-up call.

Panther: "Hey, guys, could I get a 5:15 tomorrow?"

Monkeys: "No problem, Larry. Goin' huntin'?"

Panther: "Nah. Just want to get an early start on lickin' myself."

Each morning, the howlers scream their monkey lungs out in unison, like some warped Primate Vienna Boys' Choir. The sound echoes through the trees up to four kilometres away. And when you are pure city folk who have just spent your first sleepless night in the jungle... well... it's creepier than that baby crying in the woods in *The Blair Witch Project*.

"Josh!?! Josh!!?!"

The only thing more frightening was the fact I was about to do two hours of yoga at 6 a.m.

Background: My wife has been training to be a yoga instructor for the past year. She found this trip by Googling "yoga retreat," though I believe it can also be located by Googling "Medieval torture methods."

I jest (partially). Truth is, since she started yoga, I'd been pondering trying it. Like most guys, I am about as flexible as wood. And I now routinely pull my hamstring putting on socks. So I figured a little yoga would help me pretend to be an athlete for a few years longer.

I probably should have practised a little. The jungle isn't really a place for a yoga virgin. If yogis did rookie hazing, it would probably be here.

"OK, rook! Hold that backbend! Don't worry about the scorpion climbing your inner thigh!"

There were about 15 of us. Most of them yoga instructors from Chicago and New York, so bleepin' flexible they probably just pretzeled themselves up in the suitcase to save the airfare. They had legs wrapped over shoulders, shoulders bent under butt cheeks, butt cheeks curled around biceps. There were snakes peeking in saying: "Dang, I can't even bend that!"

And then me.

My poses were unrecognizable. My Downward Dog needed to be put to sleep. My Triangle Pose looked like a rhombus. The only Yogi I resembled was... Bear.

Though I was proficient at something they call Corpse Pose, where you lie on your back at the end of the workout like you're dead. Which was close to accurate.

Yoga may be the single toughest workout I've ever had. I can see why it is one of the trendiest training regimens for NFL players. I did more than 20 hours' worth in my one week in the jungle. That's just plain nutty. By the end, I could almost touch my... knees. And I was uttering things like: "Hey, girlfriend, your asana was perfect today! I think I'll work a little Kundalini in with my Ashtanga next week, just to focus on my pranayama. Know what I'm sayin'?"

The yoga classes bookended every day. Here's some of the stuff we did in between:

ZIP-LINING: You've probably seen this on *The Amazing Race*. (Aside: Do they have to keep telling us the rules on that show? It's been on for... like 10 seasons. I believe I know "a Detour is a choice between two tasks," OK, Phil!?! I figured it out, oh, by about the second episode of Season One. And by the way, does any host in television have a better gig than Phil? He travels to every exotic spot on the planet, and while the contestants are shovelling camel dung in the desert or something, Phil probably lounges by the pool getting loaded while receiving a Thai massage. Then he gets chauffeured to his plastic mat just so he can say: "You're Team Number Three!")

Zip-lining is basically sliding along a metal clothesline through the jungle. I always figured it was one long ride, but instead there are a bunch of platforms spread through the trees. You zip from one to another. Get unfastened, refastened, and off you go. The kind of thing Tarzan would have thought of if he had a little more MacGyver in him. Some of the rides were several hundred metres long, with a good 10-storey drop. I challenge anyone to do it without yelling "Wheeeeeeeeeee!" Can't be done.

My favourite part was trash-talking the odd monkey we'd go whizzing past.

"Hey there, Maggie's cousin, check me out! If you'd only evolved a little more, this all could have been yours, sucker! Who's your Lord of the Jungle now, bee-otch! Wheeeeeeeeeeee!"

(See. Told ya.)

WHITE-WATER RAFTING: The Pacuare, Spanish for "Holy crap, I'm glad I wore a helmet!" is one of the top white-water rivers in the world. The scenery is gorgeous and there are Class 4 rapids galore.

Of course, I was stuck on raft with four women (including my girl) who weighed a total of roughly 300 pounds. This is not your ideal rafting crew. If it were Disneyland, they wouldn't have met the size requirements for the Tea Cup ride. I figured we'd hit a big wave, and just float off into the sky, like Chitty freakin' Bang Bang. Two of them could barely reach the water with their paddles. I may as well have been rafting with cats.

Not to brag, but I carried us down that river. It was heroic. I kept imagining I was Meryl Streep in *The River Wild* and Kevin Bacon had a gun to my head.

Bacon: "You get me down this river, Duthie, or you and your lady friends are dead!"

Me: "Ah, OK, Kev. But if I do, will you recreate your dance solo from *Footloose*? 'Cause man, that still kills me."

ATTEMPTING TO GET CULTURED: One day, a local guide took a handful of us to one of the most remote parts of the country, on the border of Panama. (We actually crossed the border illegally to swim in a waterfall. That would have been a great phone call to the boss: "Hey listen, about that opening night *NHL on TSN* double-header... Uh... just brainstorming here but... what about hosting it via satellite from a Panamanian jail?") We took a boat an hour upriver to visit an ancient tribe that makes raw chocolate from cacao plants. Isolated indigenous tribes aren't what they used to be. I was expecting loincloths and blow darts.

They had iPods.

THE BLACK HOLE: For our eight days in the jungle, we had no access to the outside world. No TV. No papers. No Internet. No phone. I brought one lousy *Sports Illustrated*, which I read so many times, I can recite every statistic from the "Faces in the Crowd" section. My favourite athlete is now Lori, a three-time National High School Fencing Champion from Rhode Island. She has great teeth.

This week will be an eternal sports black hole in my brain. Do not ever ask me anything about weeks two and three of the NFL season. It doesn't exist in my mind's hard drive. The Ryder Cup? I got nothin'. (Which, from what I hear, is the same way Phil Mickelson will remember it.)

What my mind retains instead are the memories of meshing body and spirit while practising an ancient art in one of the most lush, beautiful places on earth.

Oh yeah, and the fact my wife owes me one mother of a present when my birthday comes.

• • •

Postscript: I actually took up yoga full-time after that trip. And by full-time, I mean once a month or so. After five years, I can now bend over and almost touch my... thighs. Yoga has actually become very trendy with professional athletes. Yoga vacations in remote jungle huts with screaming monkeys has not.

NHL STANDINGS
SHOULD BE POINTLESS

December 2007

A couple of weeks back, when Toronto GM John Ferguson Jr. bore a striking resemblance to Sean Penn in *Dead Man Walking*, he kept desperately spewing the stat that his team was only "three games under .500." Today, he will proudly tell you his team is .500. A virtual juggernaut! Time for a Dear John letter:

Dear John,

I'm sorry to report that your Leafs are actually 12-18. That would be six games under .500.

I shouldn't pick on JFJ (his own boss, Richard Peddie, takes care of that), because every general manager and coach in the league omits the final column of the standings when spin-doctoring his team's record.

You see, NHL teams don't count overtime or shootout defeats as losses. Most of their fans don't either. Everyone pretends it's a tie, as if anything that happens after 60 minutes is just some DVD Extra.

Oh sure, when you win in OT or a shootout, it's a pure W. But losses are simply deemed "not quite wins."

"At least we got the point" has replaced "It is what it is" as the silliest quote of our (ice) time.

Pssst! That guy who dangled past your D-man and went five-hole in the first minute of overtime? That was not a skills exhibition. You LOST!

The extra point has so mangled NHL standings and altered players' psyches, sometimes they don't even know if they're slumping or streaking. Let's say Ottawa plays six games with these results: win, OT loss, loss, win, shootout loss, OT loss. One sportscaster will say: "The Sens are really slumping! They have only one win in their last five!" The next sportscaster will report: "The Sens are rolling! They have points in five of their last six!"

You need Stephen Hawking to figure this stuff out.

The solution is simple: it's time to kill hockey's version of The Rouge. Here's a radical idea: two points for a win, zero points for a loss. No in-betweens. No consolation prizes. No lovely parting gifts.

What other league rewards losing? Did the Tennessee Titans get anything for taking the Chargers to overtime on Sunday? Do the Blue Jays gain a half-game in the standings when they lose to the Yankees in 11? When Chris Bosh misses a buzzer-beater in double OT, does he say to himself "Oh well, at least we got something out of it!"?

Professional sports should be cut and dried. You win or you lose. You can't kinda-sorta lose. If a tie is like kissing your sister, a point for an OT/shootout loss is like kissing your creepy aunt with the mustache.

I don't care if you skated your J-Lo off for 65 minutes, only to be defeated in a "lousy freakin' shootout." If a shootout can decide soccer's World Cup, it can decide who gets two points and who gets none in a regular season hockey game.

One of the reasons hockey suffers in many US markets is fans can't even figure out how to read the standings. In some papers, the NHL has more columns than the stock market page: W, L, OTL, SOL, LWBPMPF (Loss When Your Best Player Was Maimed by a Philadelphia Flyer).

This is how the standings would read in my Utopian world (where, by the way, I would be reading the standings while getting a foot rub from Jessica Biel): one column for wins, one for losses, one for points. That's it. Easier to read than *Marmaduke*. Heck, you don't even need the points column. But since hockey is the only sport that has it, I'll throw the purists a bone.

The NHL, of course, will never go for this. It sees The Rouge as a way to keep lousy teams in the playoff race longer, an argument that has economic merit but reeks of desperation. General managers and coaches hate my idea because they are junkies when it comes to points.

"I'd rather play overtime for 10 minutes and only give the winner the two points," says Senators GM Bryan Murray. "If it's not settled, then one point each as it was before. But 4 on 4 and shootouts are different, and in my thinking, even if you lose, you should get a point. I'm too much of a traditionalist."

The only coach I could find who shares my distaste for the extra point is Calgary's Mike Keenan.

"I hate it. This game was made to be won or lost. No middle ground," Keenan says.

It should be noted that Keenan despises the shootout, and would prefer an overtime that started 4 on 4, and then went to 3 on 3 to decide the outcome. That has merit, but it's a whole other column. I'm just working with the tools the NHL has given me.

And the one point I'm trying to make is that you should never make one point.

There. For once, a column of mine that actually intended to be... pointless.

• • •

Postscript: My emails on this one were equally split between support and hate mail. By the way, much of the hate mail came from executives of lousy NHL teams. Keenan was fired after the 2009 season. The only coach who supported my plan... gone. It reeks of a conspiracy.

MOUNTAIN VIEW

January 2004

The highest peak in Canada is Mt. Logan, in the St. Elias mountain range in the Yukon, standing 5,950 metres or close to 20,000 feet.

The second highest, pending official measurement, is the snow-bank in front of my house.

Seriously. This sucker is huge... Gigantic... HUGANTIC!

We now refer to my front porch as "Base Camp." Last night, I let the dog out and there were three Sherpas pitching a tent. When I looked out the upstairs window this morning, I swear I saw a yeti.

You see, Mr. Plow apparently believes I'm sleeping with his wife. Or mother. For after each storm, he carefully gathers every fallen flake in the neighbourhood and piles them directly in front of our place.

For a while, I stalked him. Hiding behind the drapes at dawn, then leaping out onto the street when he showed up to drop off another couple of tons. (Note: In the circle of life, I believe this was the moment I officially became "Crazy Old Man Duthie," frightening children at the school bus stop as I shook my fist, muttering nonsensical curses while stumbling after Plowboy in my plaid jammies. All that was missing was the cane. I really must get a cane to shake.)

It was fruitless. He'd just smirk, dump and drive off. Satan in a City of Markham toque. And I was left to sit and stew, and plot vengeance before the next snowfall.

"Look, Crazy Old Man Duthie's setting traps again! Run!"

I was becoming obsessed with Plowjerk in a destructive *House of Sand and Fog* kind of way. That is, until the kid set me straight.

After school one day, my four-year-old dropped his Bob the Builder backpack off at Base Camp and started climbing. And not just any side of my snowbank: the treacherous north face.

"Nooooo!" I screamed inside my head. "You forgot your oxygen canisters!"

By dinner, he had almost reached the summit. Sir Edmund Freakin' Duthie.

Soon, the other kids in the neighbourhood had joined him, keeping one wary eye on the door for the Crazy Old Man.

But he didn't come. He just watched.

Before long, they'd fetched sleds, and were plummeting down my Everest. Then one kid brought a snowboard. Then a skateboard. Then a bike. (Really.) Suddenly, it was the Winter X Games. I envisioned a scene from *The Simpsons* trampoline episode, kids scattered across my front yard with legs and arms pointing in wrong directions. But I couldn't stop them.

And haven't since (though I did intervene when my two-year-old tried to ride down on her Big Wheel). They're back every afternoon. Heck, sometimes I even join them.

Hey, it's just like the touching end of Home Alone! *The Old Man isn't scary!*

My mountain rules! I may put in a gondola. Intrawest called. They want to build a hotel and condos at the base. I'm considering a bid for the 2006 World Alpine Championships.

Problem is, it hasn't snowed in days. It's getting icy up there. The course is faster than the Hahnenkamm. So now Crazy Old Man

Duthie and his kids sit at the window waiting for snow.

And when it falls?

Bring it on, Mr. Plow. Bring it on.

• • •

Postscript: A few mild winters followed, and our snowbank never again reached the Himalayan heights of that winter. In 2008, we moved to Aurora, a town 20 minutes further north, in the middle of a snow belt. Our new Plowguy is much less evil. He pushes everything to the centre of our cul-de-sac, forming a ginormous three-peak mountain range, which my kids have yet to summit. My youngest daughter plans on leading an expedition up the south face sometime this February. I smell a Jon Krakauer book. Pray for her.

63

GENO COMES OUT
OF THE SHADOWS

March 2009

His Pittsburgh Penguin teammates call him "Geno," but there are a
few other appropriate nicknames for Evgeni Malkin. Like, say: Robin,
Tonto, Boo Boo, Tattoo ("Zee plane!"), Garfunkel, Mr. Smithers, Ed
McMahon (or Andy Richter, if you want to be more current).

Malkin has spent the first three years of his brilliant young NHL
career being hockey's ultimate second fiddle. Drafted second... right
after Ovechkin. Arrives in Pittsburgh... right after Crosby. And he's
been stuck in that whopper of a double-shadow ever since.

"He is overshadowed, and I can never understand why," says Buffalo goalie Ryan Miller, who ranks Malkin among the most dangerous players he has ever faced. "People always seem to just gravitate
towards one or two players in a sport. Malkin is like Dwyane Wade
this year in the NBA, having an amazing season but everybody just
talks about Kobe and LeBron."

He's right. Sidney and Ovie have become the NHL's Kobe and
LeBron, at least in terms of popularity and hype. Ever since they

came into the league, "Crosby or Ovechkin?" has been the hockey equivalent of "Ginger or Mary Ann?" And either-or debates don't usually have a third option (Mrs. Howell?). But you'd better make room for one now.

Malkin is running away with the scoring race, and has led (yes, I know... with Crosby) the Penguins on a warp-speed ascent up the Eastern Conference standings. After a stirring five-point performance last Tuesday, he heard chants of "MVP! MVP!" from a smitten home crowd.

And yet, outside the Pittsburgh city limits, almost every fan-player-coach-analyst you ask about the Hart still picks Ovechkin without hesitation. (And until last week, most had Zach Parise second.) Malkin might just be the most productive afterthought the game has ever seen.

"I had a reporter ask me yesterday if I thought he was an MVP candidate, and I said 'Candidate? Are you nuts?' He's been the best player in the league all season long," says Malkin's teammate and former roommate Maxime Talbot. "He gets no attention whatsoever. It's ridiculous."

There is, of course, a logical explanation for this. Ovechkin and Crosby don't cast shadows, but eclipses. Everything Ovechkin does or says is marketing gold. He oozes charisma. Geno just doesn't have that particular gene-o.

"He's just a different person than Ovechkin," says agent JP Barry, whose firm represents Malkin and Crosby. "He's more reserved and laid back, Ovechkin is outgoing and in your face."

That contrast was clear at an after-party at the NHL All-Star weekend in Montreal. Ovechkin danced madly atop a couch in a VIP area overlooking the club, four girls in tow, several more climbing over one another looking for a chance to... umm... play on his line. Meanwhile, 30 feet away, Malkin sat quietly with a couple of friends, unnoticed and, seemingly, content that way.

Their frosty relationship (which dates back to a run-in between Ovechkin and one of Malkin's close associates at a Russian bar) did thaw that weekend, thanks to peacemaker Ilya Kovalchuk. Malkin even helped Ovechkin with his props during the skills event. But they aren't friends.

Crosby doesn't have Ovechkin's flare, either, but he also possesses something Malkin never will: Canada. In his back pocket. Sidney has been a national icon since... oh... peewee. His boy(wonder)-next-door, straight-as-an-arrow image is like porn to corporate marketers. Sid sells. And thus, he is EVERYWHERE. Malkin, with the exception of a lucrative equipment deal with Nike Bauer, has not had a single North American endorsement opportunity.

"To be fair, not many hockey players do, outside of Sid and Ovechkin," says Barry. "Evgeni just doesn't speak the language well enough yet. If you can't speak English, it's hard to do commercials. But I think the opportunities will come."

Malkin's friends say he is charming and funny, and the English is coming, slowly. His buddies and teammates used to chuckle at his replies to their texts, which would usually consist of nothing but a "K," a "$" (they have no idea what that meant) or a "Da," the Russian word for yes. Now, there are actual words in complete sentences.

(Yes, this is what we've come to. We judge someone's communication skills by the quality of their texts.)

"He is much more comfortable now," says Talbot. "We have a shootout at the end of every practice and one day he couldn't score, and I couldn't miss. He starts yelling at me 'Max, this is not possible, you cannot score, you have no hands!'"

The ability to chirp in English is not the only sign of Malkin's growing comfort. He has finally moved into his own house, after living with teammate/full-time translator Sergei Gonchar for the last two years. Gonchar was his security blanket. He discarded it. And maybe, just maybe, he is about to do the same with those two unshakeable shadows.

"Two years ago was Sid's year. Last year was Ovechkin's year. And when it is over, I believe this will be remembered as Geno's year," says Barry.

K. Da. $.

• • •

Postscript: *His agent's words proved prophetic. Malkin won the scoring race, the Stanley Cup and the Conn Smythe Trophy as playoff MVP. He also finally won over fans. In a post-game news conference during the final, Malkin repeated his line about Talbot having no hands, cracking up the assembled media—the same crowd he used to avoid at all costs. It was played over and over across North America—it was THE moment Malkin arrived as an NHL megastar.*

GO RAT-HORSE GO!

March 2003

Nowhere in my Shawn Kemp Guide to being a Sports Parent (a must-read—after all, with about a dozen kids at last count, who has more experience than the Kemper?) does it mention what is the right age to take your son or daughter to his/her first big-time sporting event.

I'm guessing that if you want them to fully comprehend just how religious an experience this is for a father, and to appreciate the bonding involved, the answer is somewhere around 37.

So, I jumped the gun by about 34 years or so by taking my boy to his first Toronto Raptors game.

Attending a professional (oh sorry, Raptors, make that semi-professional) basketball game was, by no means, his deepest preschool desire. In fact, right now, he lists as his lone goals in life:

- To become a dragon.

- To eat our house.

Hardly a guy who appreciates a good pick and roll.

Still, when the Wizards came to town last month for MJ's last Toronto appearance (*unless they meet in the playoffs—*just so you know, I stopped after writing that and giggled for several minutes at its absurdity*), I figured this was an event he needed to see. How cool will it be 15 or so years from now when he's sitting around the frat house with the boys, watching LeBron James win his seventh MVP, and they start comparing him to Jordan, and my boy says, "Hey, I saw Jordan play." They'll all go, "Wow, Duthie, you're cool!" (Which, by the way, will be the first time that phrase has been uttered in at least two generations.)

He'll just have to leave out the part of the story where he wouldn't get in the car, screaming "NOOOOO, I DON'T WANT TO WATCH THE RAT-HORSES. I WANT TO GO HOME AND WATCH *DRAGON TALES!*"

Apparently, "Rat-Horses" is what Raptors sounds like to a three-year-old. Personally, I kind of like it.

"Jared," I said, in what I now believe was my inaugural father-son speech. "A lot of Raptor [Rat-Horse] fans would probably rather watch *Dragon Tales* these days. Heck, Lenny Wilkens would probably rather watch *Dragon Tales*. But we're going anyway."

He came around. As soon as he got the popcorn. As any Over-eager-To-Make-Their-Child-A-Sports-Freak-Parent can attest: when you're three, the popcorn is all that matters.

The biggest building he'd ever been in, 18,000 screaming people, blaring funk, dancing girls, cool dinosaur animation on the big screen, and he didn't look up from the popcorn bag until midway through the second quarter. The Rat-Horses could use that kind of focus.

Only when the purple dinosaur mascot appeared did my boy spit out the last few kernels and scream with glee: "Barney!"

(Which I'm guessing is exactly what drunken mascots say to the Raptor in the mascot bar when they want to scrap.)

I tried to point out the *other* Raptors, the ones in uniform (who, coincidentally, also resemble Barney, especially on defence), but he didn't seem too interested. *What? Would you find Greg Foster entertaining?*

However, he did come up with maybe the most profound line of the year. I had bought him one of those tiny Vince Carter jerseys at halftime, and as he wore it proudly, I pointed out Vince for him, sitting in his Armani at the end of the bench.

"That's the guy whose jersey you're wearing, buddy," I said.

He stared for a moment in silence, glanced down at his shirt and then made a completely legitimate inquiry: "Why didn't you buy me a suit?"

Kid's got a point.

I spent the rest of the game trying to get him to watch Jordan. At one point, he saw MJ dribble up court and blurted out: "He got..."

Yes! He's going to say,"He got game!" Three years old and he has all the hip hoop terms down pat! That's my boy!

"... no hair!"

Or not.

For Michael's sake, it's a good thing the kid won't remember much, because the day went kind of like this:

"Son, see the no-haired guy shooting..." *Clank!* "... He's the best player..." *Airball.* "... in the history of the..." *Turnover.* "... sport."

Mike went 1-9 for two points. And the Wizards still beat the Rat-Horses by double-digits. I elected not to clip the box score for his scrapbook.

Of course, none of that seemed to matter to a kid who was wasted on popcorn and fruit punch. He ate like Brando, screamed at Barney, climbed over and under seats, and whacked half the row in front of us with those long skinny balloons they give the fans behind the baskets to wave during foul shots.

It was almost as good as *Dragon Tales.*

"Dad, can us go see the Rat-Horses again sometimes?" he asked on the ride home (yes, he used "us" instead of "we" and he always adds an "s" on "sometime"—but he insisted he not be misquoted).

"Sure, buddy," I said. *"Just please don't make me do it until they stop sucking," I thought.*

Bad day to be a Rat-Horse. Great day to be a Dad.

• • •

Postscript: *I must be a horrible father, as I don't think we've been back to a Rat-Horses game since then. I do plan on taking my two little girls to their first game this season. After all, Greg Foster is long gone, and Vince Carter is now getting injured every other game for Orlando. Toronto actually wins sometimes now. Though it likely won't matter to the kids, as long as there is popcorn, and men in purple dinosaur costumes.*

WHY'D YOU DISS HOCKEY, TIGER?

June 2008

Eldrick Woods,
111 Huge Frickin' Mansion Lane,
Jupiter, Florida, 33478

Dear Tiger,

I doubt you remember me. We have met only twice. The first time was in a clubhouse bathroom at Augusta National on the Saturday morning of the 2002 Masters. You walked in and took a spot at the urinal next to me. I was startled, tried desperately to think of something cool to say, but could only muster, "Good luck." You chuckled and answered, "Thanks, but I do this several times a day, I'll be all right."

I thought that was pretty darned funny. Oh, by the way, you won that weekend (I figure you must lose track).

Our second meeting came right after you claimed the 2005 British Open at St. Andrews, when I conned my way into a one-on-one interview with you for TSN. The only thing I remember about it, besides how friendly and laid back you were (such a contrast to the stone-faced golfing Terminator people seen on TV), was that you called me "Homeslice." Seriously. Just before the camera rolled, I said, "Congrats," and you answered, "Thanks, Homeslice." It freaked me out a little. I hadn't heard the word Homeslice since Dwayne Wayne used it on *A Different World*. Or maybe it was Rerun on *What's Happening*. You must have been joking with me again, because it would really hurt your street cred if you actually use that word regularly.

Anyway, Tiger, those two encounters mean we're pretty tight, right? So I am writing to ask you a favor.

Don't diss hockey anymore, Tiger.

You've probably heard by now your little quip last week got a lot of attention up here. You know the one. Some reporter asks you on a teleconference call who you are cheering for in the Stanley Cup Final, and you reply, "I don't really care. Ask me about the Dodgers. I don't think anybody really watches hockey anymore."

Zing!

Now, I know this is old news and you've long since moved on to that little US Open thingy you're apparently involved in this week, but I've been on the road and hadn't had a chance to share my feelings with you. So I just wanted to say: don't worry, old buddy. Your comments didn't bother me much. Knowing your zany sense of humor like I do, you were probably pulling our legs again. I'm guessing you giggled internally as soon as you said it, thinking, "This'll get my buddy Weirsy all riled up! I kill me!"

You are one wacky funster, Tig. But here's the problem: most hockey fans who aren't as close to you as I am didn't get it. You see, we puckheads get our backs up when someone knocks our game. We feel sucker-punched. So we hit back. Hockey columnists wrote scathing editorials about you. Hockey commentators ripped you. Mike Milbury came to work Tuesday in Pittsburgh begging me to let him go after you on our panel. Sorry, Tiger, I couldn't stop him.

"You know what? I'm gonna change the name now. It's gonna be Tiger Wuss!" Milbury said. "Here's a guy that took about three months to get over a simple arthroscopic surgery. You look at Ryan Malone. His face exploded with a slap shot—he's back out in 10 minutes!"

And you thought Johnny Miller was tough! Could have been worse. Milbury could have hit you with a shoe (YouTube it, Tiger, if I lost you there.)

Your comments struck a nerve because we all admire and respect you. Heck, almost all hockey players golf. And if you are fortunate enough to be a Toronto Maple Leaf, you get to play a lot. Hockey people idolize you. So when you mock their game, it hurts them. Especially when you're wrong.

Yes, I know you weren't talking about Canadians when you said no one watches. You've spent time up here. You know that if we don't watch hockey, we get deported. It's in our Constitution. But even in the US, you are off base. Didn't you see NBC's ratings for the Cup Final? Hockey is hot in the US again. We may soon catch arena football in the ratings down there. After that, who knows? Women's softball might even be within reach.

Anyway, Tiger, I just think it would be best if you left hockey alone and went back to ripping Phil Mickelson. Now, that was good comedy.

No hard feelings. We're not going to get Sidney Crosby to slam golf, just to get even. And if even you don't watch our sport, we'll keep watching yours. At least when you play. (No offense, pal, but we aren't exactly rushing home Sunday to watch Bart Bryant and Tom Pernice battle it out for the Des Moines Open.)

Signed,
Your old pal, James (Homeslice)

• • •

Postscript: *I included this column in the book just so we could all remember that simpler time, when the biggest controversy Tiger was involved in was upsetting a few hockey fans. Things have gotten a little... uhh... trickier, for him since.*

SURVEY SAYS!

November 2008

The brass of the National Hockey League Players' Association is in the midst of a full, 30-team fall tour, trying to take the pulse of its constituency on a variety of key issues.

Just out of curiosity, did you nod off during that lead? Thought so. I'm well aware that Players' Association news makes eyes glaze over faster than that design magazine your wife made you look through to pick out drapes. (That analogy comes from a very dark personal place.)

But trust me, this is important stuff. NHLPA executive director Paul Kelly and director of player affairs Glenn Healy should be commended for trying to reinvigorate the PA, and empower the players. And hey, this is novel: they aren't even spying on emails to do it!

Every NHL player is being asked to fill out a confidential survey about several key issues. Once all teams have been polled, the results will go a long way in dictating the PA's agenda.

We have obtained the questions from the survey. Though intriguing, it seems to be missing some important follow-ups. So we conducted our own more detailed NHL player poll. Here are the questions and answers from both (since results of the NHLPA survey have not been tabulated yet, we offer instead our own unofficial estimations).

ACTUAL NHLPA QUESTION:
Would you support the competition committee investigating a penalty for headshots?
Yes: 75%
No: 25%

OUR FOLLOW-UP:
Would you support a penalty for shots to Sean Avery's head?
No: 99.9%
Yes: 0.1% (Avery)

ACTUAL NHLPA QUESTION:
Do you want NHL players to participate in the Olympic Winter games after 2010?
Yes: 98%
No: 2%

OUR FOLLOW-UP:
Do you know the 2014 Olympics are in Russia?
Yes: 63%
Oh. Crap. Can I change my vote on the last question?: 37%

ACTUAL NHLPA QUESTION:
Are you in favor of grandfathering-in a mandatory visor rule?
Yes: 70%
No: 30%

OUR FOLLOW-UP:

Do some of you believe the previous question meant your grandfather is the one who would have to wear the visor?
Yes: 34%
No: 5%
You wanna go right now pencil-neck smart-ass?: 61%

ACTUAL NHLPA QUESTION:

Are you in favor of terminating the current collective bargaining after the season?
Yes: 10%
No: 90%

OUR FOLLOW-UP:

What are the 10% of you who said yes smoking!?! Do you really want to spend next season in OMSK again?!?
(I didn't actually ask that. It was more of an editorial comment.)
Wow. Very revealing. Unfortunately, that's it. The NHLPA survey is only four questions long. (Hockey players have short attention spans. Any more than four questions would require a protein shake and a rubdown.) To get a more detailed look at players' attitudes and beliefs, we added some bonus questions…

Which idea do you support to increase scoring in the NHL?
Bigger nets: 23%
Smaller goalie equipment: 26%
Drugging and kidnapping Roberto Luongo: 51%

Who or what is to blame for the current financial woes of many NHL teams?
Gary Bettman: 37%
The US economic crisis: 49%
Jason Spezza: 14% (Hey, he gets blamed for everything in Ottawa. Might as well call him out on this one, too!)

What is your biggest concern about playing in non-traditional hockey markets?
Less revenues means lower salary cap: 19%
Endorsement opportunities reduced: 15%
Hot girls in Nashville bars have no idea who I am: 66%

Would you approve of a shorter 72-game schedule?
Yes: 14%
No: 13%
Can we still get paid for 82?: 73%

Have you, at any point in your NHL career, dated Elisha Cuthbert?
Yes: 32%
No: 7 %
Hope to: 61%

• • •

Postscript: *I thought the survey was a great idea (especially my questions). But it didn't help Paul Kelly. He was fired by the NHLPA in a very controversial move at the end of August 2009. Healy resigned a few days later.*

TOTAL (LACK OF) RECALL

December 2003

This is the time of the year to reflect on the events of the past year in sport. Or so my newspaper tells me. So here goes.

Umm.

Ahhhh.

Hmm.

I got nothin'.

Wait! Mike Weir. The Masters! I remember that! And Jesse Palmer got a start for the Giants! Of course, that was an hour ago. The rest is pretty much a blur.

Truth is, I've become Guy Pearce in *Memento*. I'm Matt Damon in *The Bourne Identity*. I'm Dory the Fish in *Finding Nemo*. Sports moments happen. Sports moments are forgotten. Usually instantaneously.

When my *Sports Illustrated* arrived this week with Tim Duncan and David Robinson on the cover, hailed as Sportsmen of The Year, my immediate reaction was, *"What did they do?"* Followed shortly thereafter by, *"Oh yeah, they won... I think."*

You see, I have not a single recollection of the NBA Final. I think they might have played the Nets because the Nets always win the East and then play bug-meets-windshield in the Final, but the rest is blank. Nothing but colour bars on the plasma screen in my brain. In fact, I don't remember any moment from *any* NBA Final since Michael beat the Jazz.

And I watched them all.

It's hardly just hoops. My entire sports memory is fading faster than the Dolphins.

There was a time when I could take you batter by batter through the '92 World Series. Now, I remember about as much of the '90s as Robert Downey Jr.

My theory is when you hit a certain age... say 30... your brain is full. And from that day on, every time you save a new memory, another falls out the opposite ear, never to be retrieved.

When my beautiful baby daughter was born this summer, I believe I lost the entire second half of the '81 Superbowl. My son just skated for the first time. It was magical. There goes Leonard vs. Duran (1 *and* 2).

I suppose, in theory, it could work the other way, too. If Canada wins gold at the World Juniors this year, maybe I'll forget making out with Alison White behind the portable after Grade 8 grad.

With apologies to Marc-Andre Fleury and the gang, that would be a shame.

Alison aside, I've also become useless when it comes to recalling dates. My buddy Rod Smith (TSN *SportsCenter* anchor, not Denver Bronco receiver... although I'm extremely tight with both) is an encyclopedia. Ask him about the 1976 AFC Divisional Semi-Final, and he'll give you the stats, starting lineups and who sang the anthem.

I'm having trouble remembering what AFC stands for.

And it's getting worse. The other night as I got home from work, my neighbour asked me who won the game we aired that night. About 10 seconds of awkward silence followed, as I scanned my shrinking brain searching not only for the score, but for the two teams involved in the telecast I'd completed a half-hour earlier.

"You did the Rangers-Habs game, didn't you?" he finally offered, with a partly puzzled, partly sympathetic, partly *"What's the matter with you, freak?"* look.

"Yeah... That's right! Uhhh... The Habs won! I think."

I would love to attribute all this to the fact I have a new baby, plus two other tykes who apparently believe they are nocturnal, and thus most days look and feel like I spent the last six months with Saddam in his spider-hole.

But it's more than that.

Maybe I've lost some of my passion. Maybe because of all the money and egos, sports just isn't what it used to be for any of us. Or maybe I'm about as bright as a Hilton sister.

Anyway, if, by chance, I somehow impress you in a future column by pulling out some obscure reference to a past sporting event, you'll know what part of my memory it came from.

Google.

• • •

Postscript: *This column is the EXACT reason I wrote this book. So when future emailers ask me some obscure question about a column I wrote in 2006, I can grab the book and look it up, instead of giving my usual response of the last few years: "You sure I wrote that?"*

AARON FREAKING
WARD

February 2009

There is no better story in the NHL this year than the Boston Bruins. Wait, check that. There are no better storIES in the NHL this year. For the Bruins are not a novel, but a collection of feel-good shorts.

There is Marc Savard, the former most-forgotten superstar in hockey, finally getting his due. There is Phil Kessel, who fought cancer, and doubters, and beat them both. How about Big Z, who has put it all together and seems poised to steal the Lidstrom... err... Norris Trophy. Or Michael Ryder, from Montreal bust to Boston steal. There's new Boston folk hero Milan Lucic, or perhaps you prefer David Krejci, the "Where the heck did he come from?" kid. And don't forget Tim Thomas, whose life story is a Disney movie-in-waiting.

And somewhere near the back of the book, around page 290, there is Ottawa boy Aaron Ward.

Not a very sexy yarn, is it? He rarely makes the *SportsCenter* highlights. You'd never pick him in your pool. C'mon, with all those other Bruin tales, why would you care about a defenceman who doesn't do anything remotely spectacular on the ice?

But you have reasons. For one, he went to the same public school as you, and your Mom, a teacher, told you he was a "very interesting, boisterous boy." This amuses you, but it's still not enough. No, you talk to Aaron Ward because unlike most of the players in this league, Ward actually TALKS. And he does so without spewing a single cliché or ducking a question, which is a rather religious experience in this column business.

And when a player has three Stanley Cup rings, has been to five finals, was almost destroyed by Scotty Bowman, and once nearly scrapped with teammate Jaromir Jagr on the bench, there is plenty to talk about.

The basics: Ward grew up in Ottawa's east-end (Manor Park and Blackburn Hamlet). He played for the Gloucester Rangers and Nepean Raiders, but when he was cut from his AA team at 14, the NHL dream wasn't looking so good.

"I was thinking about quitting, but a coach named Taran Singleton (now video coach with the New Jersey Devils) talked me out of it," Ward says.

It wouldn't be the first time he'd consider quitting. He thought about it, oh, just about every second with the Detroit Red Wings, where he broke into the NHL. A certain legend named Scotty Bowman decided Ward would be his whipping boy. And, man, could Scotty whip. In fact, for years Ward thought his middle name was "freaking" (or a cousin of that word), because all he ever heard was "Aaron Freaking Ward."

"Scotty was very effective because he would strike fear in the hearts of his players by using some guys as examples. Most of the time, I was that example," Ward says. The Scotty stories are plentiful, and sadly, unrepeatable in a newspaper. Except for the odd one.

"One night in Chicago, I blocked a shot with my mouth and from the lip to the nose, I was gushing blood everywhere. As I headed to the dressing room, Scotty yelled, 'If you're not back in five, you don't play another shift.' Our doctor was about 80, so I knew there wasn't a chance that the stitches were going in that fast!"

Another night in Colorado, Forsberg and Sakic stepped on the ice, and Detroit assistant coach Dave Lewis sent Ward and his partner out.

"Scotty came running down the bench, yelling 'Jesus, Dave, are you trying to make us lose the game!?!' I was halfway across the ice, but I could hear it so clearly, I decided to save my career so I did a 180 and went back to the bench."

Ward would leave Detroit with two rings... and zero fear.

"It was a nightmare, and he never relented the whole time I was there. But in retrospect, it was the best thing for me. When I left, I knew no matter what any coach ever did or said to me, it would be child's play in comparison. It made me much tougher."

And better. From being a sixth or seventh D-man in Detroit, Ward went to Carolina, where he was on the top pairing for the Canes title run in 2005–06. Stanley was starting to follow Aaron Ward around.

The only place it lost his trail was New York, where he signed as a free agent in 2006. Ward's pet peeve is me-first players, and he's not good at hiding his disdain. He grew increasingly frustrated with Jaromir Jagr, and one night in Tampa, lost it on the bench, questioning Jagr's work ethic and leadership. Right or wrong, you don't often win dressing room fights with superstars. Ward was traded to Boston at the deadline.

"The first two or three months here, we weren't very good," he says of his first season as a Bruin. "In fact, there was nothing redeeming about our team. But that started to change last year. I think Claude [coach, Julien] gave us a system, beat it into us over and over again, so that now we know if we do it right, there's no chance we'll fail."

And so here we go again. The kid who got cut from AA, the kid who Scotty almost left curled up in the corner of the room in the fetal position, now has a legitimate chance to become only the fourth player in the expansion era to win Stanley Cups with three different teams.

Aaron freaking Ward.

• • •

Postscript: *Ward's Bruins were upset by Carolina in the second round of the playoffs that season. He became a central figure in the series after being sucker-punched by the Hurricanes Scott Walker, and then ripping Walker and the Canes in a media scrum the next day. Ward, who lives in Raleigh in the off-season, instantly became the most hated man in Carolina. He received death threats, and police stood guard outside his home. Sure enough, he was traded back to Carolina in the summer of 2009 (all is forgotten quickly in pro hockey). Ward was traded again, to Anaheim, at the 2010 trade deadline. When he retires, he plans to pursue a career in hockey broadcasting. Good call.*

BAH HUMPUCK!

October 2005

We are a nation of complainers.

We complain about the weather. "It's too cold!" "It's too hot!" (My otherwise perfect wife—always suck up before you mock—has a window of .6 degrees Celsius where she is content: 23.5 to 24.1. If it hits 24.2, she starts fanning herself and yells at me for not having a pool. If it dips to 23.4, she runs screaming for a sweater.)

We complain about our jobs. (Like last week, when the makeup artist powdered my forehead a little too firmly and I had to scream at her and make her cry. I bruise very easily.)

We complain about our family. (Thanksgiving was a prime example. It was the same old song and dance at my folks' place: "Mom, why can't Dad be here?" "We've been through this, James. He's in prison.")

But more than anything, we complain about hockey.

During the lockout, roughly 98 per cent of the emails I received were about how to fix the game. (The other 2 percent were autograph seekers, wanting to know if I could get to Gino Reda. I can't, by the way. He signs only at shows.) Newspaper columnists have made careers out of "What's wrong with hockey" rants.

But now what? What can we possibly whine about, when the game looks as good as it's ever been?

Oh, we'll find something. We always do. It's just who we are. So here's a pre-emptive strike. The first "What's Wrong With Hockey" column of the post-lockout NHL era.

1. TOO MANY GOALS: 5-4? 7-6? 8-3? This bites. In the good ol' pre-lockout days, you never feared missing a goal when you abandoned your recliner midway through the game to, you know... make a sandwich... put the kids to bed... build a deck. Now? You can't take a pee-break without missing three lead changes.

2. TOO MANY COMEBACKS: Used to be when your team led 2-1 after two periods, you could go to bed early, completely confident in victory. Heck, even the freakin' Capitals were, like, 23-1 when leading after two. And a two-goal lead? Man, a two-goal lead after one and you could flick over and watch the cougars. (No, not *Animal Planet*, you idiots. *Desperate Housewives*.) Now... 3-1, 5-2... Nothing's safe. The Kings blew a 4-0 lead on opening night. 4-0?!? In the old NHL, with a 4-0 lead, guys would be sipping martinis and getting their legs waxed on the bench. Now, you actually have to stick around... and watch the whole thing! That's way too time-consuming.

3. TOO MUCH EXCITEMENT: Remember when you could watch a game while also: paying your bills, writing your thesis, making hot passionate monkey lo... I mean... uhh... cookies. Now, the games demand your full attention. It's a multi-tasking nightmare.

4. TOO MUCH POTTY MOUTH AND SPITTING: Actually, that really hasn't changed. My Nana just wanted me to put that in.

In summary, these new rules suck. I long for the glory clutch and grab days of the past. For goalies who looked like Jabba the Hutt. For those 1-1 Minnesota-Carolina classics. Now, that was *my* NHL.

Anyway, gotta go. I'm watching Toronto-Ottawa, and the Leafs just scored three in the third to take the lead, only to see the Sens score two to retake the lead, only to have the Leafs tie it and send it to overtime, where both teams missed glorious chances, leading to a shootout featuring some of the most dynamic players in the league.

Damn game.

• • •

Postscript: It's now been five years since the new NHL rules were implemented, and the game is faster and more exciting than it has ever been. But we still complain, we still tinker. And we always will. Because it is hockey, and we are Canadian, and that is just what we do.

GETTING A BAD REP

November 2007

As you read this, I'm probably in a rink.

Doesn't matter when you are reading it: in your jammies Saturday morning, over lunch, before dinner. I'm probably in a rink. Heck, I'm writing this in a rink. I'm at Thursday hockey practice (which follows Tuesday speed skating, Wednesday game, and precedes a Friday, Saturday, Sunday tournament).

For this year, I have joined the cult known as "Rep Hockey Parent." Do not fear me. I mean you no harm.

After two years of house league, my seven-year-old boy is playing his first year of minor novice rep. He's having a ball. So, I'm thrilled for him. And terrified for me.

I love hockey, but this is nuts.

House league was Club Med compared to this. One little weeknight practice, one relaxed Saturday morning game and the rest of the weekend was all ours. We'd go to movies, take the kids to the park, do yardwork. OK, I never did yardwork.

Now? My weekends are like an episode of *The Amazing Race*.

"To complete this task, you must get your son to the rink by 8:00, your girls to gymnastics by 9:30, grab the Timbit that will be your only meal of the day, get the groceries, pick up all three kids, drop the girls at learn-to-skate and get your boy to his second game by noon. The last parent to arrive will be eliminated."

My wife and I have to book our dates six months in advance now. We're going to a movie in March. Might even go for a drink after. We're crazy like that.

And apparently, we're getting off easy! Our coach is relaxed and... sane. He never says boo if we have to miss a practice.

The next-door neighbour's boy is a 10-year-old AA player. He's on the ice five or six times a week and has nine tournaments before Christmas. All mandatory. Nine!?! That's nine Fridays off school. Nine entire weekends gone... Poooofff! Like some David Blaine trick.

And you parents with two or three kids in rep? I have no comprehension of how you do it. Can you freeze time like that guy on *Heroes*? Have you mastered teleportation? Did you clone yourselves?

Look, I enjoy going to the rink as much as anyone. There is nothing like watching your kid finally turn his patented "flick" into an actual wrist shot (I think there are a couple of Leafs who still haven't done that).

But I'm already wondering how much is too much. So, I called a couple of other dads I know to ask their opinion.

"Two to three times a week on the ice is plenty," says Martin, a father of two young boys.

"And never ever more than four a week, even in rep," adds Marty, who has two girls. "Let them do other things."

Oh, by the way. The last names of those two dads? St. Louis and Turco.

Yup. Two of the best players in the NHL never played as much kids' hockey as our little ones do today. In fact, almost every player I talk to says the same thing. Our kids are on the ice waaaay too often.

"Summer hockey especially bothers me," says Turco. "Take the ice out. I never played in the summer. I played everything else. Sure,

I missed hockey but I also never came to hate it because I'd played too much."

The goalie's right. We've all seen those little glassy-eyed, year-round hockey robots, who have had all passion for the game sucked out of them by age 10. Of course, there are some who you could put out on the ice four hours a day and it still wouldn't be enough.

So, we'll watch our boy closely to see which way he leans. If the fun of rep starts to fade, we'll happily go back to Club Med. But for now, *The Amazing Race* continues.

And we're surviving. It doesn't consume our entire life. In fact, tonight we have no hockey! We're going out!

To a team fundraiser. Wanna buy a raffle ticket?

• • •

Postscript: Three years later, we're still living the rep (no)life. The kid loves it, so we're all in. Heck, in retrospect, I had it easy back when I wrote this. Now, my daughters both do competitive indoor soccer, dance and yoga in the winters. Thankfully, there is no rep yoga. Yet. "Down dog tournament this weekend in Oakville! Bring your mats, and be there two hours early for meditation!"

BYE-BYE *SI*

December 2006

I collect next to nothing.

No hockey cards, no sports memorabilia, no used Vic Rauter powder puffs. (Jay Onrait keeps those. Creepy.) The one exception is a pile of magazines that, if set on fire, would be visible from outer space.

I kept every issue of *Sports Illustrated* since my Mom and Dad gave me a subscription for my birthday in 1981. (Along with a large monkey-puppet that my sister knit a Clemson Tigers sweater for. True story. A sad, troubling one. But true.) That's a quarter century of *SI*: 1,400-plus magazines, lugged across the country through three cities and eight moves.

It was not a collection, per se. I never laminated the covers, never displayed or hung them like some sports bar. They were simply dumped on a pile that would need its own wing on the Duthie Estate, if there were a Duthie Estate (I'd prefer a compound). Instead, they just lay in boxes, out of boxes, around boxes, taking up our entire furnace room.

There was a logical reason for this Mother-piece of packratting. When my little boy, or girls, got interested in sports, I wanted them to be able to dig through the old *SI*s. I figured it would be like opening paper time capsules of seasons and eras gone by.

I wanted them to see those wonderful covers of Michael Jordan in his prime: gravity-defying, tongue-wagging, so they wouldn't just know him as some guy on the Celebrity Golf Tour. I wanted them to read the Gary Smith pieces that could make you laugh and cry in the same paragraph, and convinced their dad to study journalism.

My wife bought that sappy story for 15 years, until she brought home a truckload of Christmas presents last Saturday, and declared the furnace room the only viable place in the house to hide them. Problem was, she could barely open the door, and had neither the energy nor Sherpa guide necessary to ascend Mount *SI*.

They had to go.

And so my children's sports library, their lifetime of joyful retro-reading, would instead amount to one afternoon with my seven-year-old boy, trying to teach him 25 years of sports history while we dumped load after load in the recycling bin.

It was a glorious few hours, gazing at those faded, dog-eared, food-smeared covers. There were images I recalled instantly: Andre Dawson and Dave Stieb in front of a Canadian flag (*THOSE CANA-DIAN CLUBS!* July 18, 1983), a steroid-swollen Tony Mandarich (*THE INCREDIBLE BULK*, April 24, 1989) and a young pre-face tattoo, pre-circus act, pre-everything Mike Tyson (*KID DYNAMITE*).

There were headlines dripping with irony. Giant cartoon heads of Sammy Sosa and Mark McGwire adorned the March 6, 2000 issue with the cover line: *ALL THE JUICE IS IN THE NL CENTRAL*. You weren't kidding!

We giggled together at Gary Nicklaus's Daisy Duke shorts (*THE NEXT NICKLAUS*, March 11, 1985). I giggled alone at *WHY CAN'T THEY RUN LIKE OJ?* (Oct. 8, 1990). That one required a little too much explaining for the boy. There were dubious predictions: *WOODEN BATS ARE DOOMED!* (July 24, 1989)… And what now seem like silly questions: *CAN THE NFL BE SAVED?* (Dec. 6, 1993). Hmm… I think maybe it'll be OK. As for *CAN THIS MAN* [Doug Flutie] *SAVE THE USFL?* (Feb. 25, 1985). Uhh... I'm thinking not.

I told the boy he could choose a couple of issues to keep. He grabbed one of the few hockey spreads we could find, featuring Tony Tanti (Nov. 21, 1983). He is now convinced that Tony Tanti is the defining hockey player of the last half-century. This brings me much amusement.

But the issue he really wanted was the 1991 College Football Preview Issue with Houston Cougar Quarterback David Klingler on the cover holding a stick of dynamite (*BOMBS AWAY!*). He immediately proclaimed Klingler his favourite athlete. For a seven-year-old, any guy who walks with a lit explosive in his hand defines cool. I haven't figured out how to break it to him that David Klingler is probably selling insurance in Austin now. I kept about 50 myself. Some Gretzky and Mario cover issues, every 49ers cover, my Perry Tuttle Clemson Tigers National Championship cover (Hey, my sister didn't knit that monkey-puppet sweater for nothing!), the Sportsmen of the Year Issues, and a Rick Reilly column on the late (Kansas City Chiefs running back) Joe Delaney, which is still the best thing I have ever read.

Oh yeah. And the Swimsuit Issues. Now those, I may laminate.

• • •

Postscript: I just hit 30 years of subscribing to Sports Illustrated. *But it's not the same anymore. I used to read it cover-to-cover the day it arrived. Now I end up with a stack of six that haven't been opened, which I'll skim through when I get a rare free hour. Who has time to read sports columns anymore? Oh wait... crap.*

THE RIGHT DUFF

October 2007

My son hates Mike Comrie. Mike Comrie ripped his heart out. Mike Comrie stole his woman.

You see, my boy is in love with Hilary Duff. Problem is, Hilary Duff is in love with Mike Comrie.

So, protective father that I am, I confront Comrie about how he has heartlessly crushed a not-quite eight-year-old who owns a Hilary Duff poster and three CDs, which I am obligated to play on the way to every one of his hockey games. Comrie just laughs and says: "Tell him I never meant to hurt him."

Sure you didn't.

But sorry, son, the guy's too nice to stay mad at. And the story is so Disney-ish, it should be a... Hilary Duff movie! Hockey star boy meets sweet Hollywood star girl (at a resort in Idaho this past July). Boy and girl go gaga over each other. Boy lights up the league in the first week of the season with girl cheering him on in the stands.

So darn sweet, it almost makes you want to puke.

After rebooting his career last season in Ottawa, Comrie signed with the Isles and has been an early-season revelation. He has four goals and seven points in five games, playing 22 minutes a night on the Islanders top line. All the while becoming a tabloid all-star:

"Hilary and fresh boy toy Mike Comrie were spotted having a romantic dinner last night at Giorgio Baldi restaurant in Santa Monica. Comrie is the center for the New York Islanders hockey team. Score!"—TMZ.com. (I particularly enjoyed the phrase "the center," as if a hockey team only has one. Oh wait, it's the Islanders. They might be right.)

"Apparently, the two are very affectionate toward one another," according to friends of Duff. *"They're always together and can't keep their hands off each other."*—GossipGirls.com. (Good to see an old-school NHLer can still clutch and grab.)

"Hilary and her new beau cuddled and danced together all night long from their perch on the third-floor VIP section overlooking the dance floor."—People.com. (... And she screamed in glee when he seamlessly transitioned from Robot to Macarena.)

Comrie laughs it all off.

"I certainly never wanted to be in the tabloids," he says. "You try to keep your privacy. But I understand her fans want to know what she's doing. It is a little strange to walk out of a restaurant and there are 25 cameras waiting for you."

Yeah, it took me a couple of years to get used to it.

You'd think a player might be distracted by all this Hollyweirdness. But Comrie is doing the opposite. He's thriving. When Duff came to see him play for the first time in the pre-season, he had four points and the game winner. (I personally believe he put her in the front row to distract the opposing goalie. Evil genius, that Comrie.)

Duff is currently shooting a movie in New Jersey, so the pair has been spending a lot of time together. You won't get many more details out of Comrie. He wants to keep the relationship as private as possible. He'd rather talk hockey.

Forget that! I talk hockey all day. I want to talk about the girl. So many questions: Does he play that "Wake Up! Wake Up!" song on his iPod before every game? Does he have a favourite *Lizzie McGuire* episode? Does he ever pull a Britney and not wear underwear on purpose to shock the paparazzi?

Sadly, there are no answers. For some silly reason, Comrie puts his relationship ahead of my disturbing curiosity. (So selfish.) But sources close to him (crap, I sound like I'm writing for *US* or *In Touch*) say the relationship is getting serious. So, I beg him for one answer. Is it serious, Mike?

"Yeah. It is. I don't think I've ever been happier in my life."

OK, now you can puke. I have to go console my son.

• • •

Postscript: Comrie cooled off, but still had a good year with the Islanders, scoring 21 goals. He was traded to Ottawa the next year, and then signed with Edmonton in the summer of 2009. But through all the uniform changes, the girlfriend has stayed the same. Comrie and Duff got engaged early in 2010. My son has moved on to Megan Fox. Give the boy credit: he has taste.

A BREAK FROM
BERTUZZI

February 18, 2004. This column was written four days after Todd Bertuzzi attacked Steve Moore on the ice in Vancouver. It was, from the standpoint of public reaction, one of the worst weeks in the history of hockey.

• • •

For a moment, forget about it.

Forget the bounty, the stalking, the sucker punch, the blood, the stretcher, the kid in the hospital, the terror his family must have felt, the outcry, the tears, the suspension, the hate mail you've gotten blaming the "evil media" and the hate-hockey mail from those fed up with the game.

Just take a minute, and log off from this whole nightmare.

So you do. You go down to your basement, where you find your boy, digging through his toy closet looking for the $2 yellow plastic hockey stick his overanxious Dad bought him while he was still in the womb.

That's weird. The boy never liked the stick. It had barely been out of the box. Oh sure, he likes sports. He'll hit golf balls in the backyard grass 'til there's no grass left. Just mounds of ugly divots. He doesn't care that his only club is a rusty right-handed Spalding junior ladies 7-iron with a baby blue grip. And he's a lefty.

He'll sneak up on you in the office and chuck the Nerf off the side of your head while you're typing, then laugh like he's funnier than Chris Rock. He'll open the basement bathroom door, stick his two-year-old sister in front of it, and fire soccer balls at her like it was the FA Cup Final.

But not the stick. Never the stick.

Maybe this is the junior kindergarten version of rebellion; his stance against the endless hockey highlights he is force-fed every morning while Dad watches *SportsCenter*, when he could be watching something profound and important. Like *Rescue Heroes*.

You've tried not to worry about it. Tried not to be one of those dads, the ones who have their kids in power skating while they are still in Pull-Ups.

"He's four, and he hasn't even had lessons yet?" they ask you, befuddled by your obvious failure as a hockey parent. But you didn't want to force him. After all, you didn't skate until you were eight. And you ended up starring on the... Blackburn Hamlet Peewee House League Champion. (OK, Consolation Champion. Point is, there's no hurry.)

And even if he never played, even if he preferred... oh, say... rhythmic gymnastics... (gulp)... you'd be supportive.

But suddenly, there he is: grabbing one of the cheap yellow sticks, handing the other to you, and making two nets out of plastic bowling pins. Game on. Sure, he only shoots backhands, misses on 80 per cent of his one-timers (actually, all he has is one-timers... no interest in that stick-handling thing yet) and figures his sister's doll's head makes a perfect puck. But, man, he's having a blast. You haven't seen his eyes light up like this since the first time he had Fruit Loops.

Later, he raids the bookshelf in your office, scanning the cover of every *NHL Media Guide* before declaring his favourite teams are the Nashville Predators and the Florida Panthers (note to sports marketers: any ferocious-looking member of the cat family works well with four-year-olds). OK, so he does refer to the Rangers as the "Power Rangers" (boy, really wrong on that one), and calls the Maple Leafs something that sounds like "Maco Leaps," but give him time.

And then it hits you. Darned if for a couple of hours, you didn't forget the whole awful week. My God, kids have a sense of timing. You half expected him to wink, and say, "I knew you needed that, Dad."

Funny, you'd just heard someone on TV say that hockey lost thousands of fans this week. Maybe. But far away from that mess, it also gained a new one.

• • •

Postscript: My son hasn't put down the stick since. Hockey is now his passion. I'll show him this someday, just to let him know how strange and wonderful his timing was. The Moore vs. Bertuzzi case was still in the Canadian civil court system at the time this book was published.

ANNA AND ME:
A LOVE STORY

September 2007

OK, technically the title should be Anna and Me: A Brief Professional Acquaintance Story. But work with me here.

If you have frequented this column through the years (you really deserve some kind of government subsidy), you will have undoubtedly noticed the author's journalistic fascination (unhealthy obsession... whatever) with a certain female Russian ex-tennis player. I Googled my own archives and found that I used the word "Kournikova" roughly as often as "the."

My devotion to the Church of Anna has faded somewhat over the last couple of years. Why? Well, I have matured as a writer, no longer relying on cheap frat boy ogling lines. Plus Jessica Biel got really hot.

Truth is, I was almost over Anna until my boss called me in the middle of my summer vacation.

"Hey, James, sorry to bug you... wondering if you could help us out with an event..."

"No Shot. Summer. Me no work."

"Oh... well, it could be fun. It's a tennis thing..."

"Don't do tennis. Only contact sports. And swimsuit competitions."

"Are you sure... they want you to be the umpire for a celebrity match with John McEnroe and Jim Courier and Carling Bassett and..."

"Legends tennis? Seriously, kill me now. I'd rather watch reruns of *Full House*."

"Oh... and Anna Kournikova will be there, too."

"I'm in. Love tennis! Whatever you need, boss! You know me... company guy all the way!"

It was destiny for us to meet. Anna dated hockey players. I am a hockey commentator.

Anna dates a singer. I often sing at weddings, after four hours of open bar. Anna is young and single. I am young (compared to... say... old people) and was once single.

I KNOW! The coincidences are so... freaky!

OK, the age gap did enter my mind. I am edging close to my "Creepy Older Guy" phase. There will come a day soon when it will be icky for me to crush on twentysomething vixens. That doesn't mean I'll stop. It'll just be icky.

And so here I am, backstage at the Roger's Cup one perfect August evening, waiting for some crappy real match to end so I can have my Anna moment.

And then suddenly, before I have time to mess up my hair to look more "dangerous" and do push-ups in the bathroom, she is standing next to me. She looks a little thinner than her last *Maxim* cover, but still fAnnatastic. Our conversation goes like this:

Me: "Hey, Anna, my name is James. I'm the guest umpire for your match tonight."

Anna: "Oh."

She is clearly into me.

Me: "So... umm... how long you in town for?"

Anna: "I fly to Austria in the morning."

Unless something... or someone... changes those plans. Heh. Heh. Know what I'm sayin'? Heh heh.

Me: "Oh, that's a quick turnaround."

The single lamest comeback of my verbal life.

Me again (she apparently felt no need to reply to the last statement): "So, I hope it's OK if I have some fun with you during the match tonight. You'll be wearing a mic, too, so you can come back at me."

Anna (confused and peeved): "I'm wearing a mic? No one told me I was wearing a mic? I can't attach a mic to this."

Then in a PG *Penthouse Forum* moment, she flips the top of her skirt over about two inches to show me how thin, and... well... unmicrophonable... it is. Magic.

And then Pooffff! she is gone (likely off to berate some official or her manager about never mentioning the mic). Some talented (and dang lucky) technician found a way to get the mic on, and a few minutes later Anna is bouncing all over the court treating the exhibition like it is the US Open Final. Throughout the match, I make several spirited attempts to win her over. My decision on every protested call is:

"Whatever Miss Kournikova says."

I tell her I took Spanish in high school. I sing her pretend-boyfriend Enrique's ballad "Hero" to her. It is incredibly sweet and beautiful (though my wife, who is in attendance, strangely chooses "pathetic and disturbing" for her description).

Anna laughs and giggles and charms the umpire and every other male in attendance. (Except maybe McEnroe, who acts as if the entire event is a prostate exam.) And yet when the match is over, she offers only the traditional umpire handshake and a half-smile, and she is gone. No hand to the ear "Call me" signal. No "Next time you're in Miami, look me up." No "I've always dreamed of meeting a married-father-of-three Canadian cable sportscaster with legs like a chicken. Let's make out."

Nothing.

And so I'm here to officially announce I'm over Anna. She's dead to me. She will never again be referenced in this space.

Ditto tennis. I'm done with tennis, too. (Unless they invite me back next year to meet Sharapova.)

• • •

Postscript: *The restraining order arrived in the mail a few weeks later. See, I knew you wouldn't forget me!*

THIS DOG'S LIFE

March 2009

The greatest athlete I ever saw, pound for pound, slept beside my bed and drank out of my toilet.

I knew my dog was a little different the first time I took him to a park in Ottawa in the spring of 1997. His tale (tail) of the tape: 10 weeks old, five inches tall, maybe three pounds, with an already impressive two-foot vertical. He figured that was more than enough to match the Rottweiler and German shepherd he went after, grabbing onto some extra fur on the latter's neck with his teeth and not letting go. It resembled the young lion trying to take down the elephant on my *Blue Planet* DVD.

My dog defined runt. His size and spunk immediately reminding me of Tanner Boyle, the short-tempered shortstop from the original *Bad News Bears* movie. And so he would become Tanner, a.k.a., "The Wonder Dog."

Tanner was a Jack Russell Terrier, the "smartest dog alive," according to Gene Hackman's character in *Crimson Tide*. I believe that throwaway screenplay line was the reason I got a Jack, despite numerous canine publications that warned against it. "Extremely high maintenance," "temperamental," "not an appropriate breed for most families," they wrote. But also, "full of character." And that was the only quote I circled.

When Tanner was six months old, on a lark we took him to a Jack Russell "trial" in a small country town near our cottage. Trials are basically track and field meets for Jacks. He was too young to compete with the Big Dawgs, so to speak (Jacks don't get very big), but this particular trial had a puppy division for dogs under a year old. There were about 20 Jack pups there, most of them from serious breeders, looking for their next champion.

The trial consisted of four events: an obstacle course, a simulated underground maze (Jacks were bred to chase foxes out of holes), a hurdles race and a straight sprint. The last two have the Jacks chasing a fake rabbit's tail on a rope to a grapefruit-sized hole in a stack of hay. First dog through the hole wins. (I believe if the Olympics adopted this idea, it would make track events much more compelling.)

That day remains one of the most bizarre, head-scratching, wonderful afternoons of my life.

Tanner won them all. Four golds (sorry, blue ribbons), Usain Bolt with a tail.

Despite the urging of several breeders at the event, Tanner would not go into full-time training. We retired him on the spot. An undefeated champion. Rocky Marciano's canine kindred. While his competitive track career was over, Tanner's sporting life was just beginning.

We moved to Vancouver in late 1997 and discovered our otherwise macho little alpha dog was afraid of water. I'd jog on the beach with him every morning, and he wouldn't go near the ocean. When my soon-to-be-wife ran a bath (for her, not him), he'd hide under the bed. That all changed the day we went deep sea fishing off English Bay, and brought the dog along (before kids, you always bring the dog along). He mostly stayed inside the boat, cowering in fear, until we reeled in the first salmon. The moment that fish flew out of the water and flopped back and forth on the floor of the boat, a bell went off in

Tanner's head: Water equals fish. Fish equals... something I must have in my mouth right now!

He spent virtually every moment of the next decade trying to catch one. The size of the body of water was irrelevant: ocean, lake, river, puddle, bathtub, sink. In Tanner's mind, all water must contain fish. Fish flop. Fish = fun.

No dog obsesses quite like a Jack. Every time I bathed the kids, he would sit on the edge of the tub, waiting for that salmon to leap out of the water and into his jaws. It would eventually happen, he figured. He'd seen it. He had proof.

He would sprint along the shoreline of our cottage lake for 14 hours a day, chasing schools of minnows. In recent years, as my son grew old enough to cast off our dock, Tanner would leap off after every cast, trying to beat the worm to the sunfish. He never did catch one. But he never stopped trying. Man could learn something about perseverance from a Jack.

Tanner had more success with rocks. Some dogs fetch balls, some fetch sticks. He fetched rocks. Not little rocks. Rocks half his size. Boulders. One day at The Beaches in Toronto, after we'd moved back east, Tanner drew a crowd of 100, all stopping to watch him "rock-fetch." He'd swim out 20 feet, dive under the water, disappear for 30 seconds, and emerge with a rock twice the size of his jaw. The crowd went nuts. I should have put a hat down and collected tips.

Tanner was a born performer. And pure clutch. We lived near Withrow Park in Toronto, which used to hold a Pet Trick Contest once a year. One summer, I discovered that along with rocks and fish, Tanner loved golf clubs. I have no idea why. Perhaps the feel of the metal against his teeth. Whatever it was, it made him nuts. I could throw him a pitching wedge and he would carry it, toss it, twirl it and generally be thrilled for hours at a time.

When I heard about the contest, I figured I'd try to teach him to hit a golf ball off a tee. We practised for a few days in the park. I'd drop the club a few feet in front of the tee, let him grab it and swing, hoping he'd make fluke contact. He might have hit the ball once in 100 tries.

I had to work the day of the contest so I gave my wife a quick tutorial on my plan and let her take over. She called me that afternoon, crying in laughter. Tanner, in front of a crowd of 500, had picked up the club, shaken it ferociously in his jaw, and knocked the ball six feet forward off the tee. Again, the crowd went ballistic. The contest was won. Tanner made page two of *The Toronto Star*, complete with a large photo of him with his pitching wedge.

Like he did with track and field, Tanner retired from golf that very day. The vet kept lecturing me that the steel was damaging his teeth (the rocks weren't helping either, but he refused to give them up).

He went out like a jock, too.

Last fall, a perfect late October Sunday, we went for a walk on a friend's farm. Tanner was in the zone, running through fields and woods, chasing squirrels and desperately hoping there might be some of that fish-infested-stuff called water around the next corner. Eleven-and-a-half years old, and still the energy of a pup.

And then he was gone.

Out of nowhere, he suffered some sort of seizure... stroke... heart attack... who knows. We never will. We raced him to the vet, holding him tight and bawling the whole way. But he was gone before we got there.

My two little girls were too young to understand. They immediately saw an opening for a hamster. My nine-year-old boy was crushed, but recovered quickly as nine-year-old boys do. My wife took it harder than expected, considering Tanner shed all over her couches and clothes, leapt on counters to steal the meals she'd cooked, and generally wreaked havoc on her house for a decade.

Me, I still miss the runt every day. He would have turned 12 this week. My youngest daughter asked me recently what dog heaven was like. I didn't have one of those eloquent answers the dads in Disney movies have. So I just told her it has tons of rocks, and the fish there are very, very slow.

• • •

Postscript: *Thirteen months after Tanner's death, we decided we were finally ready for a new dog. We brought home a Boston Terrier, and named him Buddha. Buddha doesn't fetch rocks, or hit golf balls, or fish, but he's a hoot. And the kids love him. Our favourite photo of Tanner remains the screensaver on the family computer.*